DATE DUE

THE UNIVERSITY OF CHICAGO

THE DEMAND FOR TRANSPORTATION:
REGIONAL AND COMMODITY STUDIES
IN THE UNITED STATES

DEPARTMENT OF GEOGRAPHY

RESEARCH PAPER NO. 95

By

EUGENE D. PERLE

CHICAGO · ILLINOIS

1964

This research supported in part by the Headquarters, U.S. Army Transportation Research and Engineering Command. Reproduction, translation, publication, use and disposal in whole or in part by or for the U.S. Government is permitted.

Library of Congress Catalog Card Number: 64-23589

ACKNOWLEDGMENTS

This study was conducted with financial support from the U. S. Army Transportation Research Command. Under the direction of Professor William L. Garrison this research represents a portion of the Transportation Geography Study by The Transportation Center at Northwestern University. His suggestions and criticisms during the formulation of the study and his long-term support were indispensable.

Many people both at the University of Chicago and The Transportation Center offered encouragement, advice, and general assistance in the forumulation of this study. To all of them I am sincerely grateful. Specifically, I am most indebted to Professor Brian J. L. Berry, teacher, critic, and friend. He has been intimately associated with this research from inception to completion. His suggestions and criticisms have included substantive, methodological, and editorial matters. This manuscript has been improved, substantially, under his direction. Any errors rest with the author who was unwilling to implement all suggestions tendered. Also, my gratitude to Professor Chauncy D. Harris for editorial and substantive suggestions.

Assistance was offered by Sylvia Goetz, Marie Ray, and Navinchandra Amin in the compilation of data, Robert Seidel drafted the maps, and my wife designed the cover. All analysis was performed at the University of Chicago's computing center where free time was granted for this research. To the Transportation Center at Northwestern University I express my gratitude, where the author held a Union Carbide Fellowship for the academic year 1961-1962.

To the Geography Department at the University of Chicago and my fellow students there I wish to record a special mention. They have provided and sustained a spirit of inquiry within a community of scholars. Research endeavors seem to be enhanced, appreciably, in such a rarified atmosphere.

Finally, I wish to record my lasting debt to Helen and Harry, two twentieth-century pioneers. Their sacrifice permitted their sons to receive the type of formal education they were denied.

TABLE OF CONTENTS

TABLE OF CONTENTS--<u>continued</u>

LIST OF TABLES

LIST OF TABLES--<u>continued</u>

LIST OF ILLUSTRATIONS

A NON-TECHNICAL SUMMARY

Problem

This study is concerned with the demand for freight transportation in the United States as exemplified by motor carrier and railroad behavior during the years 1956 to 1960. Specifically, it examines the relationships existing between the consumption of freight services and the price system. Of course, many different variables, such as types of service, enter into a transportation decision, but in the short run the price system operates as a primary allocative mechanism influencing such decisions. Thus, we concentrated our research on the operation of the price system as the primary demand determinant.

How have prices influenced the consumption of transport services for the entire nation and for all commodities? Does this relationship differ among commodities? Are there regional-commodity combinations which generate specific types of transportation demand? These are the kinds of questions which we are interested in answering. The order of analysis is: (1) aggregate transport demand for all commodities in the continental United States, (2) transport demand for the nation by major commodity groups, (3) total regional transport demand (all commodities taken together), and (4) individual region-commodity combinations. Thus, the study proceeds from greater to lesser levels of aggregation.

Ultimately, we are interested in understanding the consumption of transport services and their relation to regional economic structure. The movement of commodities from production locations to consumer locations involves a cost. Similarly, commodities vary in their ability to bear differing cost levels. In the long-run transport costs could affect output, but in the short run this is unlikely. How responsive transport demand will be for a given commodity is not only a function of the national or regional economy but also the competitive nature of available alternative transport modes. Furthermore, transport response will be related to the differing productive characteristics of areas as a result of regional specialization. What we are suggesting is that there are numerous transportation markets in the United States and these are all subsets of a larger national market. These individual transport markets and their consumption-price relations are what we wish to understand and relate to the mix of regional output.

Methods

Throughout the analysis the relatively well-developed field of demand theory is utilized (chapter ii). Under ordinary conditions, demand theory postulates an inverse relationship between quantities consumed and prices charged for any good given the fact that the consumer is limited by some fixed income. That is, if we raise the price of a good less of it will be consumed. But how much less is a question of response and empirical research; it is measured in terms of demand elasticities. Elasticities are measures which indicate the proportionate change in consumption of a good which results from proportionate changes in prices (see chapter ii, Elasticity,a Measure of Response). Thus, the elasticity measure is a ratio of proportions or a pure number free of units. For example, an elasticity of -1 indicates that a 10% rise in price will be associated with a 10% reduction in consumption; an elasticity of -.5 implies that a 10% rise in price will generate a 5% decrease in consumption.

The price elasticity of demand depends not only upon the price and consumption of a given good but also it depends upon the prices of available alternatives. If the price of a good or service becomes too great it is possible that consumers will shift out of that good and into a substitute which will satisfy the same set of desires. Butter and margarine, beef and pork, and coffee and tea are obvious examples of substitutable goods.

In this study we are interested in the relations between motor carrier and railroad services and whether they represent substitutable goods for all commodities transported, for certain commodities, or only in certain regions. These notions lead to the formulation of a simple demand model such as:

$$Q_i = f(P_i, P_j)$$

where Q_i is quantity consumed of transport service i, P_i is the price of that service, and P_j is the price of the alternative transport service. This says that the quantity of goods transported by a given mode is a function of the price of that means of transport and the price of the alternative means of transport. This relatively simple demand model is used throughout the study (see chapter iv, The Basic Model), and it relates the quantity consumed of a good to a set of relevant prices. By means of least squares the basic model is fitted where the estimated parameters are price elasticities. Note that quantities and prices are entered as absolute values in this model.

There is a second type of demand model which can be formulated where relative rather than absolute quantities and prices are considered (see

chapter ii, Elasticity of Substitution). In this model one is concerned with
quantity and price ratios as:

$$(Q_m/Q_r) = f(P_m/P_r)$$

where m and r refer to motor carriers and railroads and Q and P refer to quantities and prices, as above. This formulation says that the ratio of the quantity
of goods carried by motor carriers to the quantity carried by railroads is a
function of the ratio of their respective prices. Estimation of this model by
least squares yields an elasticity of intermodal substitution which indicates
the change in relative quantities carried as a function of a change in relative prices. That is, an elasticity of substitution of -1 implies that a
10% increase in the price ratio results in a 10% decrease in the consumption
ratio; an elasticity estimate of -.7 indicates a less than proportional decrease in the consumption ratio subsequent to a given rise in the price ratio.
This formulation does not specifically indicate the source of the change. For
example, an increased price ratio could result from a rise in motor carrier
price, or a decrease in railroad price, or a combination of the two. Similarly, a change in the consumption ratio can reflect a change in one of the
components or both of the components. This second model is used throughout
the analysis as well (see chapter iv, The Modified Model). At this point
it should be clear that these two simple demand models yield different but
complementary types of information. The first model relates absolute quantities and prices and treats substitutability tangentially; the latter model
focuses upon relative quantities and prices and, therefore, treats substitutability directly.

In all empirical research where estimation is the objective the
quality of results is intimately related to the types of input data utilized.
The transportation sector of the economy is one of those areas where information is either severely limited in amount or else is not available in a usable
format (see chapter iii, Data--Availability and Utility). Governmental regulation provides a rich and abundant stock of railroad information which pertains to almost all railroad movements. In terms of commodity origins, however, railroad data are reported in terms of a particular regionalization
of the nation (see Figure 1) or in terms of state-to-state movements. On
the other hand, motor carriers have not been regulated for as long a period
or as completely as have the railroads. Therefore, there is less available
information and it is less complete than for the railroads. Additionally,
motor carrier commodity origins are reported in terms of a different set
of regions than are the railroads (see Figure 2). The disparity between
commodity information for these two modes is clear when one realizes that

over 95% of all commodity movements by rail are regulated and reported while only one-fourth of the intercity commodity movements for motor carriers are regulated and reported.

The disparity in statistical regions for reporting purposes was only one of our data difficulties. More serious was the disparity in the data content. Railroad information is abundant and rich, though it is reported in differing formats. Motor carrier commodity data, however, exist in only five years, 1956-1960. The reporting regions are displayed in Figure 2 and the data include regional totals only. Furthermore, the only available information by regions is tons originated and total freight revenue. These data are reported for each commodity but pertain to the entire region. Thus, the amount and content of the motor carrier information represent our limiting constraint.

In order to ensure comparability, railroad information was assembled on tons originated and total freight revenues for each commodity from the state-to-state waybill series and aggregated into the nine motor carrier regions. This aggregation ensured that observations for railroads and motor carriers would represent similar areas (see chapter iii, Conformable Statistical Regions).

Thankfully, the commodity classifications utilized for the two transport modes are the same. Some two hundred seventy-three commodities are listed. Clearly, we are not able to examine all commodities. Fortunately, a commodity classification exists which is composed of five classes: (1) products of agriculture, (2) animals and products, (3) products of mines, (4) products of forests, and (5) manufactures and miscellaneous. All commodities are grouped into one of the five classes. Analysis proceeds with the five commodity groups. Each group is conceptually assumed to represent a homogeneous good (see chapter iii, Commodity Classification). Of course, there is great variety within each commodity class, but it would be impossible to treat all commodities individually. The reduction of commodities from two hundred seventy-three to five composite groups is admittedly an over-simplification, but it reduces the number of necessary computations to a feasible size.

At this point we can review briefly the status of data availability. Our output measure for transportation service is tons. Were there free choice we would have preferred ton-miles, but this information does not exist for motor carrier commodity origins. Of necessity we must accept tons. On the national level, though, tons and ton-miles are highly correlated. Actual prices charged for transport services are not available but total freight revenue for each commodity shipped does exist. As a surrogate for price, a revenue-per-ton measure was constructed. These two measures, tons and revenue per ton, were used throughout the analysis. In some respects these data pose problems. Total freight revenue is determined both by tons shipped and the length of haul of such shipments. Thus, the price variable used has a weight and distance component built into it. Conversely, the output measure, tons, is strictly a weight measure. Whether the use of these measures introduces some systematic bias is unknown. Not only are tons and ton-miles highly correlated on the national level but also the average length of haul for each mode has varied little over the five-year analysis period. Assuming that these national relations pertain to regions and commodities one would not expect any serious systematic bias. In any event, there is little else one can do since alternative output and price variables do not exist for both modes.

Given the state of existing data we have endeavored to construct comparable series both for the railroads and the motor carriers. In this way the results obtained reflect common measures for commodities and regions. In summary, the railroad data drawn from the waybill series represent a 1% sample of a well-defined population. On the other hand, the motor carrier data represent a total enumeration of some 25% of the motor carrier population.

With nine regions, five commodity groups, and five years of comparable data there are a total of 225 observations available for analysis. The most aggregative level of analysis treats all observations together in a national demand framework (see chapter v, "Macro Analysis") Both the basic and modified models, described above, are applied and elasticities are estimated. Of course, one expects variability among regions and commodities from a national average elasticity. This problem is examined by introducing additional variables into the two demand models. These variables represent different commodities, regions, and years (see chapter iv, Dummy Variables).

The second level of analysis treats each of the five commodity groups individually on a national basis. Thus, the total number of observations are divided into five groups of 45 observations each. Then analysis proceeds where elasticity estimates are generated for each of the two demand models for each of the five commodity groups. Once again, additional variables are introduced to account for regional and temporal variations (see chapter vi, "Meso Analysis by Commodities").

Since there are nine regions the totality of 225 observations is divided into nine groups of twenty-five observations each. Then transport-demand is estimated for each region and for all commodities in terms of the basic and modified models. Commodity and temporal variations are explicitly accounted for by the introduction of dummy variables (see chapter vii, "Meso Analysis by Regions").

Lastly, the most disaggregative level of analysis treats each commodity and region combination. Since there are nine regions and five commodity groups there are a total of forty-five transport demand combinations,
where each combination is composed of five observations, the years 1956-1960.
Estimation then proceeds through the use of the basic and modified demand
models. At this level of analysis a dummy variable for temporal variation
is included (see chapter viii, "Micro Analysis--Regions and Commodities").

Conclusions

When all commodities are grouped together in a single national demand
function it becomes apparent that there has been a persistent increase in
motor carrier tonnages and a smaller but obvious decrease in railroad tonnages
(see Table 2). This combination of mode increase and decrease results in a
division of the commodity transport market such that the consumption ratio
(motor carrier relative to railroad tonnages) has been increasing in a linear
fashion at 6% per year,[1] approximately (see Table 5). This trend effect implies that motor carriers are capturing larger relative shares of the commodity
market over time. Furthermore, the division of market shares for all commodities does not appear to be highly sensitive to the ratio of prices. In
fact, the elasticity of intermodal substitution appears to approximate -1
(see Table 5). This means that a given per cent increase in the price ratio
is offset by an equal decrease in the consumption ratio. If small changes
in the price ratio induced large compositional shifts in the transport consumption ratio one would expect a rather elastic estimate, greater than -1
in absolute value. This we do not find in spite of a persistent compositional
shift in consumption. Additionally, there is a significant commodity variability component in national transport demand (see Table 7).

In the meso analysis where demand functions are estimated for each
of the five commodity groups the persistent increase in motor carrier tonnages
and decreases for railroad tonnages is confirmed (see Tables 10 and 11).
Added to the trends in consumption are elastic estimates for forest and mine
products, mildly inelastic estimates for manufactures, and rather inelastic
estimates for animal and agricultural products (see Table 15). An elastic
estimate implies a greater than proportional shift in the consumption ratio
subsequent to a given change in the price ratio. Inelastic estimates of

---

[1] During the period of this analysis there has been a marked rise in
piggy-back traffic. Unfortunately, these movements are not tabulated
separately and, therefore, it is impossible to indicate what fraction of
this growth rate might be due to this traffic. Ostensibly, some of this
traffic would represent railroad increases as well as motor carrier increases.

intermodal substitution imply less than proportional shifts in the consumption ratio. These estimates are not unexpected since theory indicates that low valued commodities are sensitive to minor pricing variations and high value commodities are quite unresponsive to small pricing variations. Nevertheless, the verification of a theoretical concept lends creditability to our estimates. Since the transport cost associated with low valued goods will represent a large part of its final market price then such goods should be responsive to pricing alterations. Conversely, transport costs represent a small part of market price for high valued goods and, therefore, these goods should be relatively insensitive to pricing alterations. Our elasticity estimates confirm these theoretical concepts.

The shifting composition of the transportation market, from the national model, is found to be dependent upon different growth rates for modes according to absolute tonnages for commodity groups (see Tables 10 and 11). For most commodities there appear to be equal percentage increases and decreases for the motor carriers and railroads from 1956 to 1960. Yet the magnitude of such changes is quite variable, such as 7.5% for manufactures and approximately 12% for forest, mine, and animal products. Such motor carrier increases and railroad decreases generate over-all increases in the consumption ratio of 15% for manufactures and some 25% for all other goods over the 1956 to 1960 interval (see Table 15). The one exception to equal percentage changes in modes relates to agricultural products. In this case the shift in the consumption ratio results almost entirely from motor carrier increases, about 22%, rather than railroad decreases, about 4%. Apparently, the competition for high valued traffic such as manufactures, which is the most profitable commodity class for the carriers, has limited the motor carrier growth rate.

Transport demand by region, according to the modified model, yielded elastic responses in the New England, Midwestern, Rocky Mountain, and Pacific Regions; appreciable inelasticity in the Southern, Middle Atlantic, and Northwestern Regions, and mild inelasticity in the Central and Southwestern Regions (see Table 24). Though it was noted that there is a linear 6% annual growth rate of the transportation consumption ratio for the entire nation, the regional analysis indicates that such a rate is not uniform among regions. Cumulative growth rates of some 15% characterize the Midwestern and Pacific Regions; growth rates in the 20% to 30% interval characterize most other regions, and the largest growth rate, some 35%, exists in the Northwestern Region.

Perhaps the most important finding of the regional analysis relates growth rates of the consumption ratio to elasticity estimates (see Table 24).

Small cumulative rates and elastic estimates are highly correlated. Elastic
estimates of intermodal substitution imply marked compositional shifts in
consumption under minor pricing modifications. In order to retain a significant share of the market each mode must refrain from pricing itself out
of the market under elastic conditions. Thus, market share growth for the
motor carriers is limited when the elasticity of intermodal substitution
is greater than -1, in absolute value. Conversely, inelastic estimates imply
relatively unresponsive reactions to pricing alterations. Thus, under conditions of elasticity there appears to be significant competition between modes
and major increases in the ratio of relative quantities are limited, as in
the New England, Midwestern, Rocky Mountain, and Pacific Regions. On the
other hand, appreciable inelasticity is associated with rather large growth
rates, as in the Southern, Middle Atlantic, Northwestern, and Southwestern
Regions (see Table 24). Under these conditions non-price determinants become more important in explaining large growth rates and imply less effective
competition between modes.

At the least aggregative level of analysis, the individual region-
commodity combination, statistical difficulties prevented us from obtaining
meaningful elasticity estimates (see The Modified Model, chapter viii).
Nonetheless, the persistent motor carrier increases and railroad decreases
in market shares were determined with relative accuracy (see Table 33).
They seem to apply to almost all regions and most commodity groups within
regions. In spite of the unreliable nature of the elasticity estimates at
the micro level of analysis, they still indicate much variability among
the individual region-commodity combinations. This finding tends to confirm our notions about regional specialization in production and, therefore, variability between region-commodity combinations for transport demand.

In the latter part of chapter ix there is a discussion about some of
the motivations behind the design and execution of this research. This
brief discussion rests, largely, upon methodological and substantive considerations. The concluding chapter terminates then with a statement of some
of the unresolved problems generated by this study and suggests avenues for
further research based on the findings and methods of this endeavor (see
Implications, chapter ix).

CHAPTER I

INTRODUCTION

Purpose and Objective

During the past few years there has developed a renewed awareness
of the role the transportation sector of an economy plays as a pervasive influence upon economic organization and structure. Of course, the relative
importance of transportation in the developmental process has been described
repeatedly. Usually, the discussion focuses upon the induced effects of social overhead capital or the increased range of commodity markets and resource supplies due to decreased transport costs.[1] Many of the more recent
transportation studies have emphasized the role of urban transportation systems generally and travel behavior in particular as they affect locational
decisions and, hence, urban structure.[2] At the same time, as urban transportation research has increased in tempo, there has developed an increased
concern about the transportation sector on the national level. This development is primarily due to the serious policy implications which transportation has on the structure and health of the national economy.[3]

---

[1]The induced or "spillover" effects of social overhead capital are
represented widely in the literature. For examples, see: W. W. Rostow, The
Stages of Economic Growth (Cambridge: The University Press, 1961); C. P.
Kindleberger, Economic Development (New York: McGraw-Hill, 1958; and A. O.
Hirschman, The Strategy of Economic Development (New Haven: Yale University
Press, 1958). Hirschman's views on social overhead investment deviate suf-
ficiently from the "conventional wisdom" to warrant serious consideration.
Nonetheless, he acknowledges the role of induced effects stemming from such
investment.

[2]There is a rapidly growing literature in this field. For a few
examples reflecting different approaches to general questions, see: W. L.
Garrison, B. J. L. Berry et al., Studies of Highway Development and Geographic Change (Seattle: University of Washington Press, 1959); W. Y. Oi
and P. W. Shuldiner, An Analysis of Urban Travel Demands (Evanston: Northwestern University Press, 1962); W. Alonso, Location and Land Use (Cambridge: Harvard University Press, 1964); and L. Wingo, Jr., Transportation
and Urban Land (Washington: Resource for the Future, 1961).

[3]At the time of this writing (April, 1964) there is the imminent
threat, once more, of a national railroad strike. This time it required
the intervention of the President to postpone such a strike and permit some
form of mediation. Yet the objectives of labor unions and management with
regard to American railroads are sufficiently bi-polar to represent a con-
tinuing series of incidents, all of which have widespread policy overtones.

1

One might well inquire into the reasons for all this research activity on transportation, both for national and urban systems. Basically, the resources that are provided and consumed in an industrial society are not ubiquitous or free goods. They are highly localized in occurrence and rarely do they coincide spatially with major population concentrations.[1] It follows that in the production process transport costs are incurred either for procurement or distribution or both. Hence, decisions relating to industrial location and land use are intimately related to transport costs.[2] Since all commodities require some transport inputs in their production this price becomes reflected in the price of every commodity offered on the market. The crucial role of transportation as a productive input has been singled out for particular attention by location theorists, primarily, and they have forcefully advanced the case for including transportation as an explicit input in the production function.[3]

While research has increased on the relations between transportation and urban structure and transportation and industrial location, there has been a concomitant research development on intermodal competition. In the past American railroads maintained a relative monopoly in transportation, which has declined under the impact of newer and competitive transport modes more recently. This development has precipitated general concern for the future of the railroads in the face of declining traffic, both for freight and passengers.[4] Supposed cures for the railroads have included decreased taxation, increased subsidy, corporate merger, nationalization, and increased regulation to cite a few. Obviously, these "cures" display a notable lack of internal consistency. In the face of dire predictions for the railroads,

---

[1] As societies continue to urbanize the disparity between resource availability (supply) and population clusters (demand) will tend to increase. There is abundant evidence to indicate that this process is likely to continue.

[2] For an exposition relating transport costs and industrial location, see: E. M. Hoover, The Location of Economic Activity (New York: McGraw-Hill, 1948), especially Part I; A. Weber, Theory of the Location of Industries (Chicago: University of Chicago Press, 1929); and A. Losch, The Economics of Location (New Haven: Yale University Press, 1954).

[3] The most recent and best developed statements on this topic can be seen in: W. Isard, Location and Space-Economy (Cambridge: The Technology Press and New York: John Wiley, 1956), especially chapter iv.

[4] For examples of publications regarding the regulated transportation industries, see: R. S. Nelson and E. M. Johnson (eds.), Technological Change and the Future of the Railways (Evanston: The Transportation Center, 1961); also, M. Reinsburg (ed.), Private and Unregulated Carriage (Evanston: The Transportation Center, 1963).

particularly, there seems to be little incisive research in progress into the determinants of transportation demand and, more specifically, the demand for railroad services.[1]

This study is directed at the demand for freight movements by railroads and motor carriers. Particular policies are neither criticized nor proposed, but the analysis has been conducted in an objective fashion. Hopefully the results may be of some use for public policy formulation.

Traditionally, the type of research conducted in the transportation field has been quite sharply demarcated along the artificial delimitations of academic disciplines. For example, geographers have emphasized the supply side of equilibrium analysis or the types of spatial patterns that emerge from the operation of the market mechanism.[2] This emphasis has rested largely upon production sites, available resources, and the transport requirements needed to deliver goods to market. Postulated relationships between transport inputs and locational decisions have involved consumer demand only tangentially.[3] Recently, though, efforts have been directed to a more analytical treatment of transportation development, structure, and locational decision-making.[4]

On the other hand, economists have placed much of their research efforts on the demand side of analysis. Their efforts have resulted in a body of theory and empirical findings relating consumer demand to production and trade. However, almost all of the demand literature has been concerned with

---

[1] A notable exception to this statement is: J. R. Meyer, M. J. Peck et al., The Economics of Competition in the Transportation Industries (Cambridge: Harvard University Press, 1960).

[2] In geography transportation research has concentrated almost exclusively on functional characteristics, flows, and use. These topics pertain most directly to the supply side of analysis. For examples, see: E. L. Ullman, American Commodity Flow (Seattle: University of Washington Press, 1957); and W. H. Wallace, "Railroad Traffic Densities and Patterns," Annals, Association of American Geographers, XLVIII (December, 1958), 352-374.

[3] The major exception involves transportation studies concerned with central place theory. For a review and commentary on the theory, see: B. J. L. Berry and A. Pred, Central Place Studies. A Bibliography of Theory and Applications (Philadelphia: Regional Science Research Institute, 1961).

[4] For examples see: P. R. Gould, The Development of the Transportation Pattern in Ghana (Evanston: Northwestern University, Studies in Geography, Number 5, 1960); K. J. Kansky, Structure of Transportation Networks (Chicago: University of Chicago, Department of Geography, Research Paper Number 84, 1963); and Forrest R. Pitts (ed.), Urban Systems and Economic Development (Eugene: University of Oregon, School of Business Administration, 1962).

consumer perishables, though it includes many commodities.[1] Only in the past few years has the emphasis shifted, though slowly. Studies dealing with the demand for consumer durables and services are starting to appear and as this trend continues the body of demand literature will achieve a more equitable balance.[2]

The present study brings some demand theory into the transportation research field. Preliminary investigations indicated that the situation with regard to freight commodity movement presented many interesting problems for empirical testing.[3] An additional attraction stems from the view that public utterances about the state of freight traffic in American transportation seemed less grounded in substance (and theory) than the passenger field. We confined our efforts, therefore, to demand for freight transportation. More precisely, our concern is with railroads and motor carriers only.

The movement of commodities from production locations to consumer locations involves a cost, obviously. But the ability of different commodities to bear differing cost levels is not so obvious. In the long run transport costs could seriously affect commodity output, but in the short run this is unlikely. Since railroads are no longer in a pre-eminent position regarding the transportation of goods to market, they are not completely free in setting price levels. How responsive railroad demand will be for a given commodity is not only a function of the state of the national economy or regional economy but also the competitive nature of available alternative modes. An added difficulty for analysis centers upon the differing productive characteristics of areas due to regional specialization.[4] Out interest

---

[1]For many examples of demand studies dealing with a variety of comodities, see: R. J. Foote, _Analytical Tools for Studying Demand and Price Structures_ (Washington: U. S. Department of Agriculture, 1958), Handbook Number 146.

[2]The best example of a volume of consumer durable studies is: A. C. Harberger (ed.), _The Demand for Durable Goods_ (Chicago: University of Chicago Press, 1960).

[3]E. D. Perle, "Time Series Analysis of Transportation Development: A Pilot Study of the Demand for Transportation in the United States," A report submitted to the U. S. Army Transportation Research Command by The Transportation Center at Northwestern University under contract: DA-44-177-TC-685, October 1962. Also, a second study by the same author, "The Demand for Transportation: A Comparative View," _ibid._, November, 1963.

[4]For a discussion of regional specialization in location and production together with avenues of analysis, see: W. Isard, _Methods of Regional Analysis_ (Cambridge: The Technology Press and New York: John Wiley, 1960).

is centered not solely on national aggregative demand. It is concerned with the demand for railroad and motor carrier services for particular commodities in different regions of the United States. As such, it is more disaggregative than many demand studies,[1] but all commodities cannot be included for analysis. Rather than single out one or two commodities for study we have chosen to group many commodities into classes and treat each class as a homogeneous good.[2]

Market economies operate under a price system and the object of prices is to allocate resources. One of the central determinants for the demand of any good is its market price. At the same time there are many behavioral determinants of demand which may be more important in the long run, such as a cultural value system, religious and dietary taboos, educational training, and the like. In the short run, however, the price system operates as the primary allocative mechanism in the determination of consumptive choices. It follows that prices also operate to allocate market shares in the short run. Although the expectations for railroads and motor carriers may be highly dependent upon long-run behavioral or technological considerations, in the short run the price system is the primary demand determinant. These notions have been expressed elsewhere, as

> The volume carried in each traffic class is determined by the total tonnage output of the component commodities and by the share of the total carried by the railroads. For the limited time period involved in this analysis, railroad rates will probably have little effect on industrial output. They will, however, significantly determine the railroad share, which is a function of the comparative course of rail and non-rail rates and of the elasticity of intermodal substitution.[3]

This study attempts to estimate the determinants of railroad and motor carrier demand. More exactly, it is concerned with demand behavior as a function of the price mechanism. Transportation demand is analyzed for the entire nation, for regions in the United States, and for commodity groups.

Organization

Chapter ii is concerned with the theory of consumer and market demand. It has been included to lay a theoretical foundation for the sub-

---

[1]Most demand studied refer to national demand for a given commodity since commodity markets are usually delimited for the nation as a unit. Alternatively, demand studies are concerned with questions of international trade. Here again the issues refer to a nation's demand.

[2]This is a potentially dangerous procedure since it implies that all members of a class are clearly defined, internally homogeneous, and differentiable from members of other classes. No claim is made that we have achieved optimal grouping for commodities. A discussion of the commodity classification used is included in chapter iii.

[3]M. J. Roberts, "Maximum Freight Rate Regulation and Railroad Earnings Control," Land Economics, XXXV (1959), 128. Emphasis added.

stantive materials which follow. No attempt has been made to make this review mathematically rigorous or exhaustive. Rather, the intention is to present some of the basic characteristics of demand theory as they now exist, neither adding to nor modifying the existing theoretical structure. For those well grounded in price theory this chapter will seem to treat a complex topic too lightly, while those unaccustomed to the material will find it somewhat complex, perhaps. As such, the chapter will not be necessary for the former group of readers. Material presented has been designed for the latter group of readers, though, so that they may better be able to follow the use of theoretical notions which are utilized in the substantive analyses which follow.

Three demand models are reviewed in chapter iii, followed by a discussion of the data used in the study. Since transportation inputs are required for the production of all commodities and since they are services rather than tangible goods, the demand for transportation is derived. That is, transport services are not desired, usually, for their own sake. Normally, consumers demand commodities for which some transport inputs are required in production. Therefore, the demand for transportation is derived from the demands for commodities. The models reviewed are all theoretically applicable to a study of transport demand; they are derived demand models. They are presented and discussed as potential guides for the generation of a transport demand model. Each model is discussed in terms of its essential components and problems, both conceptually and operationally.

Later in the chapter a discussion follows concerning the stock of available data, what data sets were used and how, the nature of their treatment, and the integration of the available data with the three derived demand models previously presented. As is true with most empirical research, the format of the available data did not correspond with our desires. Nevertheless, measures were taken to ensure comparability between railroad and motor carrier information so that the substantive analyses rest upon a common foundation. All this is discussed fully.

In chapter iv the emphasis shifts from foundation materials and issues to topics and problems associated with the estimation of demand functions. Hence, this material is technical and methodological in nature. Though the discussion contained in the chapter could have been phrased in a more general context, it is confined to issues particularly relevant to estimating transport demand. The chapter closes with a discussion of the model adopted for empirical estimation. At this point the reader will be able to compare the adopted model with the three derived demand models presented earlier. Moreover, the type of adopted model chosen will be quite clear at this stage since derived demand models, data sources and limitations, and estimation topics have been covered already.

Estimation of functions begins in chapter v, where the nation is treated as a unit and demand is estimated for all commodities together. Here our intention is to estimate national transportation demand by mode and between modes for all commodities shipped. Conceptually, this could be viewed as a problem comprising one region, the nation, with annual data for commodities and prices. Such a formulation has been avoided because of statistical difficulties and the masking effect of individual commodity and regional variations in national demand. Rather we have taken the basic input data from individual regions and commodity groups and aggregated them into a national data set. Then estimation proceeds with variables entered to account for regional and commodity variations. This is the most aggregative level of analysis in the entire study.

The next two chapters, chapters vi and vii, treat transportation demand at an intermediate level of analysis. The former chapter examines transport demand by commodities with regional and temporal variations included, while the latter chapter estimates transport demand by region with commodity and temporal effects taken into account. Conceptually, the commodity analysis is a national analysis in that it examines transport demand for the entire nation, by mode and between modes. Yet it is sub-national in the sense that separate demand functions are estimated for individual commodities. In this sense the commodity analysis is less aggregative than the analysis of chapter v, where all commodities are considered together. Throughout the commodity analysis regional and temporal variations are considered. A more truly intermediate level of analysis is conducted in chapter vii, where transport demand is estimated by region rather than for the entire nation. Though estimates are obtained for all commodities in a given region effects due to commodity and temporal variations are explicitly included.

Lastly, the least aggregative level of analysis is carried out at the individual region and commodity level in chapter viii. For each region and commodity combination transport demand is estimated and temporal effects are included explicitly. Estimates obtained at this level of analysis are comparable to those of previous chapters. This comparability ensures that the variability of estimates discovered in the more aggregative levels of analysis may be examined more explicitly since such variations are due, primarily, to particular regional specializations in production.

The concluding section, chapter viii, serves as a summary in which some of the more pertinent findings of the study are drawn together. Results which may have important policy implications are noted and topics for further related research are suggested.

CHAPTER II

ELEMENTS OF DEMAND THEORY

Demand theory attempts to explain the behavior of consumers in the market place, and is particularly concerned with the process by which consumers make choices from a range of avilable commodities on the market at a given point in time.[1] Classical or neo-classical theory begins with the notion of a utility function which makes an individual's satisfaction dependent upon the set of goods that he consumes.[2] By this reasoning, utility is a function of the quantities of goods purchased or consumed, where a rational consumer prefers more of all commodities to less, or

$$U = f(Q_1, Q_2, Q_3 \ldots Q_n).$$ (1.1)

From the utility function the next step involves deducing a set of indifference curves, each one of which define the locus of combinations of goods yielding the same level of utility or satisfaction under a set of prices prevailing in the market.

Utility, Price, and Income

When a consumer attempts to purchase a bundle of goods he not only faces a set of prices established in the market place but also he must operate under a certain fixed budget or income. Now the problem becomes one of allocation or maximizing utility, U, in the face of a given set of prices and a budget constraint, where total expenditure equals total income:

---

[1] The most comprehensive single source on demand theory, known to the author, is H. Wold and L. Jureen, Demand Analysis (New York: John Wiley, 1953). Many good economics textbooks present demand theory, as well. Those particularly recommended, depending upon one's level of sophistication, are: L. R. Klein, An Introduction to Econometrics (Englewood Cliffs: Prentice-Hall, 1962); R. H. Leftwich, The Price System and Resource Allocation (New York: Holt, Rinehart, and Winston, 1961); G. J. Stigler, The Theory of Price (New York: The Macmillan Company, 1952); W. J. Baumol, Economic Theory and Operations Analysis (Englewood Cliffs: Prentice-Hall, 1961); J. M. Henderson and R. E. Quandt, Microeconomic Theory (New York: McGraw-Hill, 1958).

[2] This presentation will utilize the utility function and indifference map constructs. It should be mentioned that there are several avenues leading to similar conclusions in demand analysis. For a highly readable and concise presentation of classical, neo-classical, and revealed preference approaches to demand analysis, see: Baumol, op. cit., chapter viii.

$$\sum_{i=1}^{n} P_i Q_i = Y , \quad (i = 1, 2, \ldots n) \qquad (1.2)$$

where P is price, Q is quantity, and Y is income. For a given set of prices, $(p_1, p_2, p_3, \ldots p_n)$ maximization of utility implies that the ratio of prices must be equal to the ratio of their respective marginal utilities, or

$$\frac{dQ_i}{dQ_j} = \frac{\text{marginal utility of } i}{\text{marginal utility of } j} = \frac{P_i}{P_j} \qquad (1.3)$$

where (dQ_i/dQ_j) refers to the change in quantity of good i with respect to a change in quantity of good j.[1]

The ratio of marginal utilities is determined by the slope of an indifference curve representing two commodities, where any one such curve defines a given level of utility with respect to a combination of prices. In order to maximize utility under a budget constraint and a set of prices there must be a unique point where the slope of the budget line is equal to the slope of the indifference curve. This is, of course, where the budget line and the indifference curve are tangent. Since prices are assumed to be positive, $p_i > 0$, and indifference curves are convex to the origin, then the slopes of a set of indifference curves and their tangents must be negative.[2] Thus, for a given income and a given set of prices the consumer

---

[1] See Henderson and Quandt, op. cit., pp. 11-13 and Klein, op. cit., pp. 19-20.

[2] Take the total differential of the utility function with respect to two goods, say Q_1 and Q_2: $dU = f_1 dQ_1 + f_2 dQ_2$. Setting $dU = 0$, then

$$f_1 dQ_1 + f_2 dQ_2 = 0, \quad \text{or} \quad -\frac{dQ_2}{dQ_1} = \frac{f_1}{f_2}$$

where $-(dQ_2/dQ_1)$ is the rate of commodity substitution or the marginal rate of substitution of Q_1 for Q_2. It is apparent that this rate is equal to the ratio of marginal utilities, f_1 and f_2. Now at the point of tangency the slope of the price line and that of the indifference curve must be equal, by definition. Obviously, the slope of the budget line is equal to the ratio of the two prices, P_1 and P_2, whereas the slope of the indifference curve is equal to the ratio of the marginal rates of substitution. But since the ratio of the marginal rates of substitution is equal to the ratio of the marginal utilties, then

$$\frac{P_1}{P_2} = \frac{f_1}{f_2} .$$

See Baumol, op. cit., pp. 153-160.

maximizes his utility if and only if he selects that combination of goods
which locates a unique point of tangency between his indifference curve
and his budget constraint.

A marginal utility relation, such as equation 1.3, if extended to
numerous goods would provide a system of N-1 relationships linking quantities
consumed and relative prices. With the addition of a budget constraint there
would be N equations. Under ordinary conditions such a system of equations
can be solved such that each quantity is expressed as a function of all prices
and income. The resulting set of equations can be represented symbolically
as:

$$Q_1 = f\left(\frac{P_2}{P_1}, \frac{P_3}{P_1}, \ldots \frac{P_n}{P_1}, \frac{y}{P_1}\right)$$

$$Q_2 = f\left(\frac{P_1}{P_2}, \frac{P_3}{P_2}, \ldots \frac{P_n}{P_2}, \frac{y}{P_2}\right)$$

$$\cdot \qquad \qquad \qquad \qquad \qquad \qquad (1.4)$$

$$\cdot$$

$$Q_n = f\left(\frac{P_1}{P_n}, \frac{P_2}{P_n}, \ldots \frac{P_{n-1}}{P_n}, \frac{y}{P_n}\right)$$

where the quantity of any good demanded depends upon all the relative prices
and real income. These relations are the demand functions of economic theory.

We have arrived at the stage where a consumer's demand for a commodity
can be determined, given his income and all other prices. It now becomes relevant
to inquire about the effect upon demand of changes in prices and/or income.
So far, the discussion of utility maximization has involved the first order
conditions for our system of marginal equations. If this equation system is
further differentiated in order to examine the effects of price and income
changes separately, then a final equation may be deduced which is known as
the Slutsky equation:[1]

$$\frac{dQ_x}{dP_x} = \left(\frac{dQ_x}{dP_x}\right)_{u = constant} - Q_x\left(\frac{dQ_x}{dY}\right)_{prices = constant} \qquad (1.5)$$

The left-hand portion of the equation (dQ_x/dP_x), indicates the rate of change
of consumption of X with respect to changes in its own price, P_x, while every-
thing else is held constant. This rate of change is seen to be composed of
two parts. The first component, (dQ_x/dP_x) u = constant, represents the change
in consumption of X due to the substitution effect while the second term,
- $Q_x(dQ_x/dY)$ prices = constant, represents the change in consumption of X

---

[1] See Henderson and Quandt, op. cit., pp. 24-26.

due to the income effect. That is, if the price of X increases one would expect some decrease in the consumption of X, but such behavior is decomposable into two effects. The substitution effect causes the consumer to substitute relatively lower priced goods for the one whose price has risen in order to maintain utility. But in order to maintain utility he must receive an income compensation since his real income is relatively less subsequent to the rise in price. The income effect indicates the consumer's consumption reaction due to the change in income when prices remain constant. After a price alteration a new position of equilibrium consumption will be established. The income effect represents the difference between a consumption position simply due to a substitution effect, a movement along a given indifference curve, and the new position of equilibrium consumption, which involves a shift to another curve.

Several additional inferences come from the Slutsky equation. First, the direction of the substitution effect is always negative. This means that if income is continuously adjusted so that the consumer realizes the same level of utility, then a price rise will be associated with a decrease in consumption. Hence, the association between price and quantity is negative, the usual form of the demand curve. On the other hand, we cannot be so certain about the direction of the income effect. In fact, it may be either positive or negative. If it is positive and its absolute value is sufficiently large to make equation 1.5 positive, then the commodity in question is said to be an "inferior good." This indicates that as real income rises the consumer wishes to spend less and less on the commodity concerned. Also, if the price of Q_x falls then purchases of Q_x will fall as well. If real income rises and the consumer wishes to spend more on the commodity in question, that commodity is known as a "superior good." In the real world most commodities are found to be "superior goods," which is the same as saying that the substitution effect is usually more intense than is the income effect. The existence of good substitutes for the commodity faced with a price increase will further decrease the income effect. The existence of "inferior goods" represents exceptional cases, in the main.

It is interesting to carry this presentation just a bit farther and indicate the implications for consumption of X given a price change in Y. It can be shown that the substitution effect on the ith commodity resulting from a price change in the jth commodity is the same as the substitution effect on the jth commodity resulting from a price change in the ith commodity, ceteris paribus. In short, the substitution effects are symmetrical. If the quantity of X demanded increases as the price of Y increases,

(dQ_x/dP_y) u = constant > 0, the two commodities are known as substitutes.
Given a price increase in Y we would expect a decrease in the consumption
of Y. If this decreased consumption of Y is countered by an increased consumption of X, then X and Y are substitutes. Both goods can satisfy the
same need on the part of the consumer and may be substituted one for the
other. If the quantity of X demanded decreases as the price of Y increases
(dQ_x/dP_y) u = constant < 0, then these two goods are known as complements.
As the price of Y increases we expect decreased consumption of Y. If this
decreased consumption of Y is paralleled by a decreased consumption of X
then these two goods are complements; they are consumed jointly in the satisfaction of a given need and there is no substitution between the two.
The notions of substitutable and complementary goods refer to cross substitution effects.[1]

Elasticity--A Measure of Response

The demands for a set of commodities can be represented by a system
of equations similar to equation 1.4; quantity is a function of all relevant prices, income, and other meaningful variables, $Q_i = f(P_1, P_2, \cdots P_n,$
y, z). The partial derivatives of such a function indicate the variations
in demand as one of the independent variables changes, all others remaining
constant. Normally, the partial derivatives with respect to own price will
be negative, the usual demand situation. With respect to alternative prices
and income, the derivative may be either positive or negative, as indicated
in the previous section. These rates of change, the derivatives, are often
cumbersome to interpret since they refer to differing units of measurement
and, therefore, are not easily comparable.

It is possible to estimate derivatives with respect to prices and
income and to compare them if the individual measurement units are replaced
by derivatives expressed in a common measure. Such is the role of the
elasticity concept. Thus, price and income elasticities are the measures
associated with the Slutsky equation, equation 1.5, while cross price
elasticities are associated with complementary and substitutable goods.

The partial elasticity of demand for good Q_i with respect to its
own price, called the price elasticity of demand, is:

$$N_{ii} = \frac{dQ_i}{dQ_i} \cdot \frac{P_i}{Q_i} = \frac{d(\log Q_i)}{d(\log P_i)} \tag{1.6}$$

---

[1]For a discussion of cross effects, see, Henderson and Quandt,
op. cit., pp. 29-30, and Leftwich, op. cit., pp. 64-66, 74-76.

This expression measures the rate of proportional decrease (increase) of demand for commodity i in terms of proportional increases (decreases) in the price of i.[1] Since this measure results from comparing percentage changes in both numerator and denominator, it is free of the original measurement units; therefore, it is a pure number or measure. In similar fashion the partial derivatives with respect to alternative prices and income can be analyzed in terms of elasticities. Thus, a cross elasticity of demand would be:

$$N_{ij} = \frac{dQ_i}{dP_j} \cdot \frac{P_j}{P_i} = \frac{d(\log Q_i)}{d(\log P_j)} \qquad (1.7)$$

where N_{ij} indicates the rate of change of demand for Q_i with respect to a change in the price of P_j. Whether commodities i and j are substitutes or complements depends upon the sign associated with the derivative or with the elasticity measure. An income elasticity of demand would follow a similar formulation in which the demand for commodity i would be $d(\log Q_i)$/ $d(\log Y)$, which is usually positive.

In practice, we collect sets of data on prices and quantities which result from market behavior over some time span.[2] Because a time dimension is now introduced we do not expect all other things to remain equal; ceteris paribus assumptions of theory are not met. Other variables are changing over a time horizon and may be related to demand behavior. Therefore, the simple inverse relationship between price and quantity may not exist in the data as collected. Often, this problem can be solved by making the relationship more complex, introducing additional variables which may be influencing the true demand function over time to give the apparently aberrent price - quantity relationship. Insofar as this situation is true, a simple relationship between quantity and price, such as:

$$Q_i = f(P_i) \qquad (1.8)$$

---

[1] For an elucidation of the elasticity concept and its characteristics see Baumol, op. cit., pp. 140-148, and R. G. D. Allen, Mathematical Analysis for Economists (New York: St. Martin's Press, 1960), pp. 251-264.

[2] We will not enter into a discussion concerning the problems associated with time series and cross-sectional samples. For discussion of these issues, see Klein, op. cit., pp. 52-74. For purposes of this study, which will become apparent later, it is advisable to introduce some concepts dealing with time series analysis at this juncture. Note the introduction of market demand here, though the previous discussion has been in terms of the individual consumer. This shift is discussed briefly at the end of the present section, but see Wold, op. cit., chapter vii.

may require modification. One alternative is to begin the analysis using a
multivariate relationship in order to account explicitly for the influence
of other variables, for example:

$$Q_1 = A + b_1P_1 + b_2P_2 \ldots + b_nP_n + c_1Y + c_iZ_i \tag{1.9}$$

where quantity demanded, Q_1, depends upon its own price, P_1, the prices of
alternative goods, $P_2 \ldots P_n$, consumer or market income, Y, and other relevant variables, Z_i.

Though equation 1.9 has been written in a linear additive fashion,
demand theory does not indicate such a specific form. Whether a demand function is linear or not is theoretically unknown before analysis; such determination is one of the objectives of empirical research. As a matter of
convenience demand functions often are estimated such that the parametric
structure is linear. In empirical estimation a balance must be found in
the convenience - realism mix. If linearity does not sacrifice realism then
it is easier to work with linear functions, both in terms of computational
ease and parametric interpretation. Therefore, one tries to keep demand functions linear in the parameters, if possible. In many cases the curvature
associated with a demand function can be handled through a simple transformation to a linear function for purposes of estimation.[1] If the realistic relation is

$$Q_i = A\left(\frac{P_1}{P_0}\right)^{b_1} \left(\frac{P_2}{P_0}\right)^{b_2} \ldots \left(\frac{P_n}{P_0}\right)^{b_n}\left(\frac{y_n}{P_0}\right)^{c_1} \tag{1.10}$$

then a simple logarithmic transformation will yield

$$\text{Log } Q_i = \text{Log } A + b_1\text{Log}(p_1/p_0) + b_2\text{Log}(p_2/p_0) \ldots$$
$$+ b_n\text{Log}(p_n/p_0) + c_1\text{Log}(y_n/p_0) \tag{1.11}$$

which is linear in the parameters. If one estimates elasticity parameters
in terms of equation 1.10 the elasticity measure will not be invariant, but
will vary along the function. Alternatively, estimation of a logarithmic
function such as equation 1.11 will yield elasticity measures of the constant variety such that they will be invariant along the function. Thus,
comparison of constant elasticity measures is enhanced, being independent
of the point of measurement.

---

[1]For examples of alternative demand functions, see Allen, op. cit.,
p. 114.

So far we have been concerned with theoretical aspects of individual
consumer demand and have introduced the concept of market demand, in passing,
in the present section. The elasticity of market demand is defined as the
relative change in consumption of a good in response to a given relative
change in price. In definitional terms this concept is quite analogous to
individual consumer demand. Since market demand elasticity is

$$N_{ii} = \left(\frac{dQ_i}{dP_i}\right)\left(\frac{P_i}{Q_i}\right) = F'(P)\frac{P_i}{Q_i} \qquad (1.12)$$

it is easily seen that the demand of a market, $Q = F(P)$, is simply an aggregation of individual demands, $q_i = f(p_i)$. If there are N individual
consumers, then

$$Q = \sum_{i=1}^{n} q_i = \sum_{i=1}^{n} f(p_i) = F(P) \qquad (1.13)$$

Let n_{ii} indicate the elasticity of demand for the ith individual with respect to some commodity. Then the elasticity of market demand for that commodity, N_{ii}, is a weighted average of the individual elasticities, n_{ii}, where
the weights represent the share of the total market demand consumed by the
i^{th} consumer, or

$$N = \sum_{i=1}^{n} \left(\frac{q_i}{Q}\right) n_i \qquad (1.14)$$

Elasticity of Substitution

In the previous section it was shown how a linear function can be
formed in order to estimate or represent the demand for a commodity, largely
on the basis of a quantity-price relation. If there is reason to believe
the relation extends beyond a simple quantity-price relation, then additional
variables can be introduced explicitly; moreover, this type of formulation
results in a set of estimated parameters including own price, cross price,
and income elasticities of demand.

If we are dealing with two commodities which are competitive to
some extent, there is an alternative estimation formulation available. This
additional estimation procedure utilizes another elasticity concept, the
elasticity of substitution, which measures the extent to which two goods can
be substituted.[1] Thus, the elasticity of substitution refers to the rela-

---

[1] This discussion of substitution elasticity is based largely upon
A.C. Harberger, "Some Evidence on the International Price Mechanism,"
Journal of Political Economy, LXV (December 1957), 506-521, and R. E. Zelder,
"The Elasticity of Demand for Exports, 1921-1938" (unpublished Ph.D. dis-
sertation, Department of Economics, University of Chicago, September, 1955).

tive mix or trade-off between competitive goods and is denoted by:

$$N_{12} = \frac{d(Q_1/Q_2)}{d(P_1/P_2)} \cdot \frac{P_1/P_2}{Q_1/Q_2} = \frac{d(\log Q_1/Q_2)}{d(\log P_1/P_2)} \qquad (1.15)$$

where Q_1 and Q_2 are the quantities and P_1 and P_2 are the prices of the two
commodities demanded. As equation 1.15 shows, this elasticity concept links
quantity and price ratios. In terms of an equation with a constant elasticity
measure, we take a linear logarithmic form as:

$$\text{Log}(Q_1/Q_2) = \text{Log } A + b\text{Log}(P_1/P_2) \qquad (1.16)$$

where the price ratio coefficient, $b = N_{12}$, is the elasticity of substitution. It represents the proportional change of the ratio of two quantities
with respect to a unit change in the ratio of their respective prices. This
is an example of an a priori combination of variables in which one parameter,
b, expresses the relationship existing between four variables.

It is surprising, no doubt, to observe the lack of an income term
in equation 1.16 when compared with equation 1.11. If two goods, x and y,
have similar income elasticities then the quantity ratio, (Q_1/Q_2), will be
little affected by income changes. If some variable is omitted from equation 1.15, such as income, and it has an effect on the respective quantities demanded then such a variable will tend to shift the relationship between the quantity and price ratios. This will not preclude obtaining an
unbiased estimate of N_{12} if the shift variable is not highly correlated
with the price ratio.

If commodities x and y have dissimilar income elasticities but the
price ratio is not highly correlated with income, then we should expect a
poor fit in our empirical estimation procedure, but no bias. Biased estimates of N_{12} occur only if the price ratio is highly correlated with income, or the omitted variable. Thus, we expect unbiased and efficient estimates of N_{12} if the two commodities have similar income elasticities and
income is uncorrelated with the price ratio; if income elasticities are
dissimilar for x and y and the price ratio is uncorrelated with income,
we expect unbiased but inefficient estimates of N_{12}, the elasticity of
substitution.

Now it can be demonstrated that the elasticity of substitution is
related to own price and cross price elasticities of demand for the two
goods. Rewriting equation 1.15 yields

$$N_{12} = \frac{\partial \text{ Log } Q_1 - \partial \text{ Log } Q_2}{\partial \text{ (Log } P_1 - \text{ Log } P_2)} \qquad (1.17)$$

where N_{12} is the elasticity of substitution between commodities 1 and 2. It is apparent that this elasticity is unaffected by the source of the change in the price ratio, (P_1/P_2). Stated differently, a given percentage decrease (increase) in P_1 has the same effect on the quantity ratio, (Q_1/Q_2), as an equal percentage increase (decrease) in P_2. Thus, we can write equation 1.17 in terms of two separate equations as:

$$N_{12} = \frac{\partial \text{Log } Q_1 - \partial \text{Log } Q_2}{\partial \text{Log } P_1} = N_{11} - N_{21} \qquad (1.18)$$

or

$$N_{12} = -\frac{\partial \text{Log } Q_1 - \partial \text{Log } Q_2}{\partial \text{Log } P_2} = N_{22} - N_{12} \qquad (1.19)$$

where N_{11} and N_{22} are own price elasticities (see equation 1.6) and N_{12} and N_{21} are cross elasticities of demand (see equation 1.7). Therefore, in a market where commodities 1 and 2 are the only meaningful substitutes for each other, then $N_{1n} = N_{n1} = 0$, where n is any other commodity.

CHAPTER III

MODELS AND DATA

In a modern economy it would be difficult, indeed, to conceive of
many commodities which do not require some transportation services in their
production and distribution. Because of such dependence transportation is
an integral part of the production process. Of course, the demand for any
input in production and/or distribution is a derived demand; that is, such
an item or service is wanted not for itself alone but for the utility it
will impart to a good. This is true of the usual case of factors of production, and transportation is no exception. Though transportation demand may
be categorized into intermediate and final demand sectors, as with goods,
such a delimitation seems rather arbitrary for this kind of service.
Furthermore, such a categorization is not crucial for analysis. Irrespective of the procedure with which we delimit derived demands, it seems
clear that freight transportation demand will vary considerably depending
upon the commodities produced and their final demands. For commodities of
low value transport inputs may represent a significant share of final
prices. On the other hand, transport inputs typically account for a
smaller fraction of the final prices on high valued goods.

Dimensionality

A firm's demand for transportation hardly can be summarized adequately by one single measure, such as ton-miles or tons. Instead, one
must consider the character of transportation services and the elements
that enter into its composition. Conceptually, it is possible to delimit
two broad categories in describing transportation: (1) those factors related to the process of physical movement and distribution, and (2) those
characteristics associated with the quality of service. The first group
is amenable to measurement and may be represented by price, length of
haul, frequency of shipments, speed of carriage, and other related variables. The second category refers to the service features of transportation such as perishability, delivery scheduling, flexibility of operations, incidence of damage, and convenience; these components are in-
tangible, in the main, and not easily quantifiable.

Because of the diverse components entering into transportation

18

offerings, each mode and each trip within a mode offers a unique mix of
services. A long run model of transportation demand would have to consider
the qualitative or service features of transportation as well as the performance variables. They may be of significant importance in understanding
secular change associated with intermodal competition and the fluctuations
of market shares. In the short run, however, many of these variables have
little or no measurable effect.

Clearly, transportation is a multi-dimensional service. Of
course, most goods and services are multi-dimensional to some degree, but
it appears that transportation exhibits much dimensionality. Because of
this characteristic it is desirable, theoretically, to analyze each movement
between a pair of points separately. Given the final demand for a good at
one location and its supply at another location, then it is possible to derive the transportation demand, as in the usual factor case. Such an approach becomes exceedingly cumbersome when dealing with numerous commodities
and numerous locations. In an effort to circumvent this difficulty, it is
assumed, usually, that freight transportation by a given mode is a homogeneous service. Thus, transportation becomes a homogeneous input in the production process in order to move goods between points of production and points
of consumption.

One Product--Two Locations

Assume a two-point economy with production at one site, A, and
consumption at the other site, B. Only one product is being produced in
our "Robinson Crusoe" world and it has to be transported from A to B.
Therefore, one unit of output (product) will require AB miles of transport
service. Since there is a product demand at B and a product supply at A, we
can derive a transportation demand function over the interval. Yet, the
equilibrium shipment of goods will also depend upon the available supply
of transportation between A and B. Now in such a situation we have two
markets to consider. One is a product market with its concomitant demand and
the other a transportation market with its derived demand. Goods will move
from production to consumption locations until the cost differential between
markets represents the cost of transfer, alone. At this stage spatial price
equilibrium has been achieved.[1] Given movement of goods between locations,

---

[1]For examples of spatial price equilibrium, see the following:
R. L. Morrill and W. L. Garrison, "Projections of Interregional Patterns
of Trade in Wheat and Flour,"Economic Geography, XXXVI (April, 1960), 116-
126; P. A. Samuelson, "Spatial Price Equilibrium and Linear Programming,"
American Economic Review, XLII (1952), 283-303; S. Enke, "Equilibrium
among Spatially Separated Markets: Solution by Electric Analogue,"
Econometrica, XVIII (1951), 40-47.

the transportation price for the commodity would be $P_T = P_b - P_a$, where P_b is price at b, P_a is price at a, and P_T is the price of transfer. This is the price per unit of shipping Q_1 units of product a distance of AB miles. Therefore, the total transportation bill will be $(P_T)(Q_1)$.

One Product--Multiple Locations

The analysis can be extended to multiple locations and one product. If we aggregate over regions it is possible to derive a regional demand and a regional supply function for a given commodity. This aggregation is a simple horizontal summation of each producer and each consumer in region i. Having obtained regional demand and supply functions, the transportation demand in region i can be derived in a fashion similar to the one good-two location discussion above. This procedure could be replicated for each commodity in each region; the transportation demand curves obtained, by region, would be summed horizontally and the result would be a total transportation demand function. The foregoing process would involve deriving the transportation demand in each region for each commodity and horizontal summation over commodities would result in a total transportation demand function by region. On the other hand, summation over regions would yield a total transportation demand function for a given commodity. This formulation implicitly considers the demand for freight transportation as the derived demand from the final demands for j commodities in n regions, with separate estimates of each.

Multiple Products--Multiple Locations

Multiple products or commodities and multiple locations permit an alternative method of analysis, one which utilizes the concept of excess demand.[1] We are interested in the production of that service called freight transportation; such production represents the output of sets of firms organized into discrete transport modes. Thereby, total transportation services are provided by a relatively small number of producer groups. The total market demand, though derived, can be divided amongst this small

---

[1] The following model corresponds to one presented by: H. Benishay and G. R. Whitaker, Jr., "Effects of Differential Taxation on the Various Modes of Transportation: Part I, Demand for Freight Transportation," Paper read before the Econometric Society, Summer, 1963. An alternative model which is similar is: C. E. Ferguson and M. Polasek, "The Elasticity of Import Demand for Raw Apparel Wool in the United States," Econometrica, XXX (October, 1962), 670-699.

set of producers or modes, such that each mode is faced with a partial demand function. Therefore, a set of equations representing total market demand, the supply function for each mode, and a balance equation would sum-
marize the entire system. From such a system, the excess demand function
for each mode may be derived as

$$q_1 = Q_d - S_2 - S_3 \ldots - S_n$$

$$q_2 = Q_d - S_1 - S_3 \ldots - S_n \qquad (3.1)$$

.

.

$$q_n = Q_d - S_1 - S_2 \ldots - S_{n-1}$$

where q is the demand for a particular mode, Q is the total market demand,
and S is the supply forthcoming by mode. This system of equations expresses
the transport demand for any mode as the residual capture between total market demand and the sum of the supplies of alternative modes. Thus, given
the total demand function for transport and the separate supply functions,
the demand by mode can be estimated.

The foregoing system requires a simultaneous solution approach,
total transport demand, and a set of separate functions, by mode. These
are rather stringent conditions to meet, in practice. In fact, we have not
been able to utilize this approach in the present study, due to our inability to meet the input requirements of such a model.

One Firm--Multiple Products

There is a third type of derived demand model which relates transportation demand to commodity output.[1] For the moment assume we have information by firm. Since transportation is an input in production and/or
distribution, the amount of transportation consumed by a firm might be
viewed as a function of firm output as: $D_T = f(X)$, where D_T is transportation demand and X is output quantity. Such a function could be fitted in
a linear format such that the proportionality between transport demand and
product output would be estimated. If all firms were single product producers the relation might be quite realistic. Though transport demand may
be highly correlated with firm output, as seems reasonable, this simple

---

[1]This model is fully discussed by F. M. Fisher, A Study in Econometrics: The Demand for Electricity in the United States (Amsterdam:
North Holland Publishing Company, 1962), chapter iv.

formulation assumes output is somehow exogenously determined. In fact, output itself is a variable in the system and may be dependent, largely, upon transportation cost considerations. Moreover, the real world economy is composed, primarily, of few single-product firms. If a firm is multi-product then consumption of transportation and composition of output mix will be highly dependent upon input or factor prices. Briefly, costs may be one of the pervasive determinants of output size and composition. The previous formulation of demand as a function of output alone takes little account of such determination.

Since transportation input information is not readily available by firm we have to resort to an aggregation process and presently we shall treat aggregation over products. The transport output ratio, an input-output ratio of transport cost input relative to unit quantity output, will vary with each product in a multi-product firm. Given a price rise in transportation inputs, which is passed on to the consumer in product price, the transport intensive products will be most elastic in the multi-product firm. Therefore, there will be a shift out of the transport intensive products and into the less transport intensive products. If we wish to maintain the same level of output quantity after the price rise then the composition of such output will, obviously, differ from output composition before the price change. Not only will product composition alter but also there will be an absolute decrease in transportation inputs. The result of this type of shift subsequent to a price rise represents a substitution in demand rather than in production.

Essentially, the previous argument of the nature and direction of substitution does not depend upon passing the price rise on to the consumer. Assume the firm absorbs the transportation price rise internally. Now transport intensive products become less profitable relative to other products. Therefore, the firm shifts out of the former and into the latter; resulting product composition is similar to the previous case. In the present instance, there has been product substitution and input substitution only indirectly. Though this latter substitution shift may be described differently than the earlier case, the outcome is seen to be the same; namely, substitution out of transport intensive products and into less transport intensive products, resulting in an absolute decrease of transport demand.

In an effort to account for transportation demand in light of both output and cost considerations, we introduce a transport demand function which expresses demand as a function of output size as well as the real cost of unit transportation inputs:

$$D_i = A_i + b_i X_i P_i + U_i \qquad (3.2)$$

where D_i is total transportation demand for firm i, X_i is an output index for the multi-product firm, P_i is the real cost of unit transport inputs, and U_i is an error term. This function, equation 3.2, indicates the total transport demand by firm as a function of its output quantity and unit transport prices. This is a transport demand function by firm with aggregation over products.

Multiple Firms--Multiple Products

The second case concerns aggregation over firms. Of course, each firm will be producing a set of products, but not all such sets will necessarily be the same.[1] For the present, assume all firms produce the same output mix under a fixed technology, but firm sizes may vary. In terms of equation 3.2, we are saying that the b_i's are equal for all firms (constant technology) but the A_i's (output size or capacity) are free to vary. In order to evaluate differing plant capacities we shall compare each firm relative to the smallest firm such that a set of ratios will result as A_i/a_i, where A_i is the size capacity of any firm and a_i is the capacity of the smallest firm of the set. Choose a group of firms which produce the same output mix under a given technology and call this set I which will number N_{It} at time t, where the smallest capacity member of I is a_i. At any moment of time summation over all such firms in the set yields:

$$D_{It} = N_{It} A + b X_{It} P_{It} + U_{It} \qquad (3.3)$$

where $D_{It} = \Sigma D_{it}$, $X_{It} = \Sigma X_{it}$, $b = b_i$, and $P_{It} = P_i$ for all i in I. Let the capacity output of the minimum size firm be x and let the capacity output of I at time t be X_{It}. Then,

$$N_{It} = X_{It}/X \qquad (3.4)$$

will hold, approximately. From equations 3.2 through 3.4 and the accompanying argument, it follows that the long run demand for transportation for the set of firms I with fixed technology and fixed A_i for firm size will be:

$$D_{It} = (A/x + b P_{It}) X_{It} + U_{It} \qquad (3.5)$$

---

[1]Product diversity complicates analysis. Nevertheless, the essence of the following argument remains unchanged.

Conceptually, the first model presented was the least difficult to handle. But, it requires supply and demand information by commodity in order to derive a transportation demand function. Though the conceptual simplicity is appealing, the informational inputs are enormous and the number of computational operations very large. The second model presented requires supply information by mode and total transportation demand in order to estimate the partial or excess demand functions for each mode. This input information, also, is quite restrictive. The last model, represented by equations 3.2-3.5, requires less input information than the previous two. Nevertheless, the last model requires transport consumption and price information together with product output quantities, irrespective of whether one aggregates over products or firms.

Unfortunately, it has not been possible to utilize any one of the three models, as formally presented here in our substantive discussion. Information scarcity precluded making any of the three models fully operational. Nevertheless, the model used most closely resembles the first model presented in this chapter. This resemblance is due to our primary concern with estimating transportation demands for commodities and for regions.

Data--Availability and Utility

In any study dealing with estimation or hypothesis testing "real world" information must be gathered for analysis. This is the most problematic part of empirical research. Often, information does not exist or is not available in a desirable format. Commonly, data limitations and reliability problems may be very real. This cannot be used as an excuse to do no empirical research at all, however. There are many serious questions and problems demanding answers, transportation included, which cannot wait until all the requisite data are available. Most probably, the day will never come when we are fully content with available, reliable data. Rather than decry present difficulties because of data limitations, which will be all too apparent in what follows, we shall describe the types of materials available and how they have been utilized in the present study.

Surface freight transportation is our primary focus and we have limited that category to railroad and motor carrier freight movements only. The single reliable source of railroad and motor carrier transportation data in the United States is the Interstate Commerce Commission. Due to the relatively lengthy history of governmental regulation of American railroads there is a considerable stock of available information about their services and commodity movements. On the other hand, motor carriers have neither such a long history of operation nor have they been so highly regulated as the railroads. Consequently, motor carrier information is much more limited.[1]

Virtually all of the freight carried by American railroads is accounted for, in terms of both traffic and financial information. This abundance of railroad information is due, largely, to their common carrier characteristics and concomitant regulation. In fact, over 95% of all originated rail freight traffic is carried by Class I railroads.[2]

Conversely, motor carrier commodity statistics cover only those operations which are labelled as Class I common and contract carriers.[3] Unfortunately, the Class I motor carriers account for only one-fourth, approximately, of the total ton-miles performed by all motor carriers.[4] The remainder is performed mainly by private carriers and the "grey area operators."[5] Thus, the available railroad information closely approximates a total enumeration while the motor carrier statistics are a sample.

Initially, one might think the relative paucity of motor carrier information to be defeating. Though data scarcity for motor carriers does represent an impediment it is not thought to be insurmountable for our purposes. Even though only one-third of the total ton-miles are performed by the regulated carriers, approximately three-fourths of the total ton-miles are performed by the long distance or inter-city haulers; there is some evidence which suggests that many of the regulated carriers would be in the inter-city category.[6] In short, the available stock of data seems to cover the inter-city commodity movements fairly well, for both railroads and motor carriers.

---

[1]For an introduction into available transport statistics see: U.S. Interstate Commerce Commission, Transport Statistics in the United States, Part I: Railroads, Part 7: Motor Carriers, annually.

[2]U.S., I.C.C., op. cit. Classes are defined according to operating revenues. Since 1956 Class I railroads have operating revenues equal to or exceeding three million dollars.

[3]Class I motor carriers are delimited according to operating revenues, too. Since 1957 Class I carriers of property have revenues equal to or exceeding one million dollars.

[4]U.S., Interstate Commerce Commission, Bureau of Transport Economics and Statistics, Intercity Ton-Miles, 1939-1959, Statement number 6103, April 1961.

[5]Grey area operations are illegal. See: U.S., Interstate Commerce Commission, Bureau of Transport Economics and Statistics, Grey Area of Transportation Operations, Statement number 6010, 1957.

[6]U.S., Interstate Commerce Commission, Truck Traffic on Main Rural Roads, 1955, Statement number 5710, July 1957.

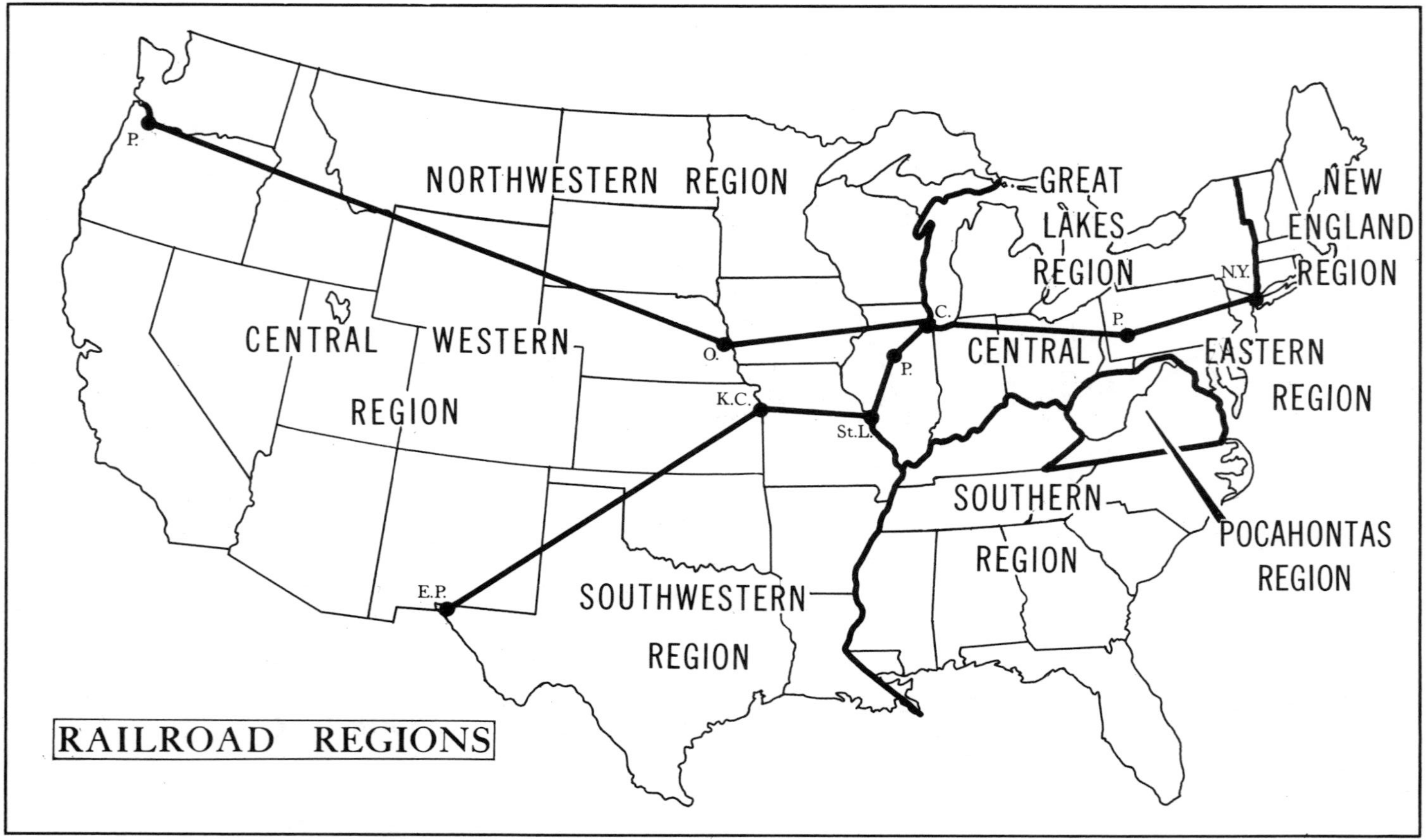

RAILROAD REGIONS

Figure 1: Railroad Regions

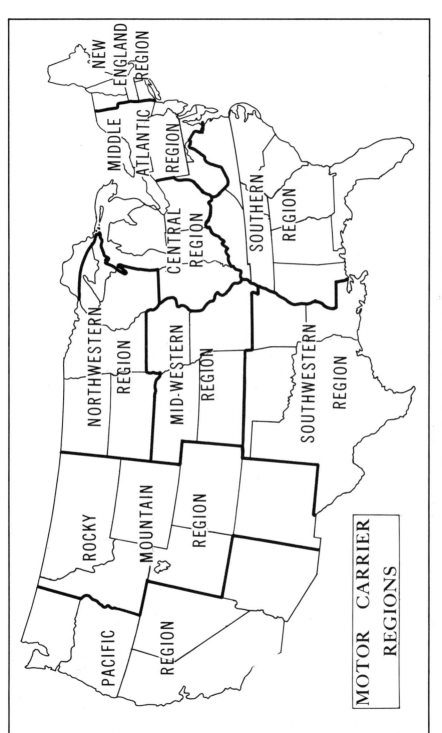

— Figure 2: Motor Carrier Regions

Statistical Regions--Railroad and Motor Carrier

Though the over-all coverage of commodity movements, with all its shortcomings, may seem acceptable, the comparability of data leaves much to be desired. Railroad commodity statistics are gathered and reported in terms of two districts, eastern and western, of which the former includes five regions and the latter includes three. Figure 1 indicates the railroad statistical regions and districts.[1] Obviously, the New England and Southern regions conform, largely, to groupings of states; the other regions reflect individual company marketing territories. No other data-gathering agency collects material on such a regional classification. Therefore, the railroad data lack comparability with other measures of the economy.

Motor carrier commodity statistics are collected and reported in terms of an entirely different set of regional units. Figure 2 displays the areal units used for reporting commodity movements for the motor carriers. Reference to Figure 2 indicates that there are nine regions used as statistical units, each of which is composed of a group of states. Since the data set does conform to political units it is comparable with many other measures of the economy, but not with the railroad regionalization, as is apparent from Figure 1. Furthermore, the data available for both railroads and motor carriers are regional totals, and greater disaggregation is not possible.

If these two data sets represented total availability the objective of this study would be doomed from the start. Fortunately, one additional data set exists for the railroads, the Interstate Commerce Commission waybill analyses.[2] The waybill series offers several possibilities since they report railroad commodity movements in terms of (1) national aggregates, (2) classification territories which are different than the regions of Figure 1 or Figure 2, and (3) state-to-state movements. Since our comparative study requires data of the most disaggregative kind for both commodities and regions, the state-to-state waybill series was the only railroad data set which offered any measures of utility.

---

[1]For railroad freight data see: U.S., Interstate Commerce Commission, Bureau of Transport Economics and Statistics, Freight Commodity Statistics: Class I Railroads in the United States, annual.

[2]U.S. Interstate Commerce Commission, Waybill Statistics, Their History and Use, Statement number 543, February, 1954.

Conformable Statistical Regions

At this point it should be quite clear that there is an abundance of railroad commodity information, though it exists in many diverse formats. On the other hand, motor carrier commodity statistics are exceedingly scarce. In fact, they exist in only one format as to regionalization (see Figure 2), and they cover only five years, 1956 through 1960 inclusive. Furthermore, the motor carrier data are more limited than the railroad data in terms of content. They include information as to tons originated, tons terminated, and total freight revenue for each commodity by regional totals only.[1] It is, thus, the availability and content of the motor carrier commodity statistics that impose the most limiting constraint.

In order to examine the comparative behavior of two surface modes, rail and motor carrier, it was necessary to aggregate the available railroad data to conform to the available motor carrier data, the limiting case. In so doing we discarded, no doubt, much useful information concerning the railroads; however, information discarded could not have been used comparatively nor verified exogenously. Since the motor carrier statistics refer to regional totals (see Figure 2) and the regions are composed of groups of states, railroad information was drawn from the state-to-state waybill series and aggregated into regional groupings conformable with those of the motor carriers. That is, commodity data on tons originated and total freight revenue for such originating traffics were aggregated from a state basis to a regional basis, where the regions are depicted as in Figure 2. By this process we were able to generate two sets of commodity data, one for railroads and one for motor carriers, which refer to a similar set of nine regions; therefore, we have comparable observational areal units.[2]

Commodity Classification

Thankfully, the commodity classification utilized for the railroad waybill series is exactly the same as the commodity classification utilized in the motor carrier statistics. The classification includes some two

---

[1]U.S., Interstate Commerce Commission, Bureau of Transport Economics and Statistics, Motor Carrier Freight Commodity Statistics: Class I Common and Contract Carriers of Property, annual, 1956-1960.

[2]Note that the upper peninsula of Michigan is included in the Northwestern Region in Figure 2, the motor carrier regions. Aggregation of state-to-state railroad data pertains to the entire state. Therefore, there is a slight discrepancy between the data for Michigan. This discrepancy is thought to be of minor consequence.

hundred seventy-three commodities subsumed under five broad commodity groups, though the individual commodities are reported separately.[1] Given such a large number of individual commodities, it is impractical to estimate demand by commodity, whether nationally or regionally. Alternatively, all commodities could be grouped together and demand estimated by region. Neither of these alternatives fulfills our objective; clearly, a compromise is the only tractable solution. Therefore, we have aggregated individual commodities into the five classes utilized in the I.C.C. classification system. This aggregation process serves to reduce the number of commodities considered from two hundred seventy-three to five. Though such a reduction may seem large, it reduces the number of necessary computations to a feasible size.

This review of the available data serves to accentuate the data scarcity problem. Nevertheless, we have indicated the decisions taken to make demand estimation, comparatively, a feasible objective. Yet, it should be apparent that the data sets available do not provide the totality of input information needed to utilize any of the three basic models presented in the beginning of this chapter. Modification of those desirable models has been necessary in light of available input materials.

---

[1]The five major groupings and the number of individual commodities included in each category, approximately, are

Products of Agriculture	55
Animals and Products	24
Products of Mines	24
Products of Forests	10
Manufactures and Miscellaneous ..	160
Total	273

The state-to-state series is issued annually in separate volumes for each of the five major commodity groups.

CHAPTER IV

ESTIMATION TOPICS AND THE ADOPTED MODEL

Some Variables

The presentation of demand theory in chapter ii together with the derived demand models of chapter iii seem to present few conceptual problems. The theory and the models seem quite unambiguous. When dealing with demand for a well-defined commodity the unit of output is usually intuitively obvious. In the present study we are concerned with the production of a service, commodity transportation, which is so multi-dimensional that the definition of an output unit does seem unclear. Is a ton of commodity "A" the same as a ton of commodity "B"? Is a one-mile movement of coal the same as a one-mile movement of pillows? Is a cubic foot of grain similar to a cubic foot of toys? In short, specifying the output unit of freight transportation poses many definitional problems.[1] Weight, distance, and volume are the most important characteristics associated with freight and there is no single measure known to the author which adequately includes all three. Often, ton-miles (a distance-weight measure) is utilized as the most desirable unit.[2] Our review of available data in chapter iii indicated that this measure is unavailable on a comparative basis. Thus, of necessity, we shall have to utilize tons as our measure of output or consumption.[3]

In the demand functions previously specified, relative prices served to allocate consumptive choices subject to a budget or income constraint.[4] If tons are used as the measure of transportation consumption, then dollars per ton or cents per ton would be the appropriate price variable. Moreover, income represents a constraint to the consumer in terms of final demands.

---

[1]G. W. Wilson, "On the Output Unit in Transportation," Land Economics, XXXV (August, 1959), 266-276.

[2]For a discussion of desirable output units, see: H. Barger, The Transportation Industries 1889-1946 (New York: National Bureau of Economic Research, 1951), pp. 24-27 and 64-69.

[3]This is not viewed as being overly serious because tons and ton-miles are highly correlated nationally. For individual regions and commodities, though, this information is not available.

[4]Refers to demand functions both in chapters ii and iii.

It has been indicated that transportation is a derived demand, the common factor case, and not a final demand. As such, the question of including an income term in a transportation demand function seems to present some doubt. If it were possible to separate transport consumption into intermediate and final demands, then the inclusion of an income constraint would be allocated to the final demands sector. In fact, such a procedure is obviated since no such delimitation of transport inputs exists.

We have argued that most freight transportation represents intermediate demands and these demands represent inputs to the firm. If this be true, there is no particular need for an income term in a transport demand function, since the firm does not operate subject to an income constraint.[1] But, the firm does operate subject to a profit constraint or a business expectation constraint. Perhaps, therefore, some measure of business profitability or business activity would be an appropriate consideration. Obviously, expansion or contraction of economic activity, whether regionally or nationally, would be expected to cause shifts in transport demand since it is a derived demand. One would expect, therefore, that transportation demand and commodity output to be positively correlated, both regionally and nationally. Thus, inclusion of a term representing economic activity or business profitability does seem justified.[2]

Collinearity

In studies dealing with time series data account must be taken of temporal effects. If there are rapid transitions of one sort or another, then a discontinuity variable may be introduced into the model. For example, if we knew that one type of economic organization pertained to the first k years of a series and another type of organization pertained to the follow-n-k years, then a discontinuity variable may be appropriate. Zeros would be entered for the first k years and ones for the remaining n-k years, indicative of the fact that economic organization had altered. In terms of transportation one could apply this technique with a series extending before and after the introduction of commercial aircraft. Alternatively, if the effects are of the slow moving secular change variety then some type

---

[1]Any good economics textbook on microeconomics will cover the theory of the firm. For example, see: Baumol, op. cit., chapter x.

[2]A length of haul variable would have been desirable too, but this information does not exist for motor carriers by regions or commodity group. Nationally, though, the average length of haul for the modes has been relatively constant from 1956-1960. We assume, therefore, that length of haul is rather fixed.

of time trend may be introduced, in the absence of known causal variables.
Both of these techniques attempt to account for temporal changes explicitly.

Because of the nature of time series data such analysis gives rise,
quite often, to serial correlation and multi-collinearity problems. The
former problem is evident from the non-independence of a set of observations at time periods t, t+1, t+2, ... t+n.[1] Similarly, if a model is
used such as

$$Q_i = A + B_1 P_i + \Sigma B_n P_n + c_1 Y + c_2 T \qquad (4.1)$$

where P is price, Y is income, and T is time, then collinearity questions
arise due to the association between income and time. If Y and T are highly
correlated two problems may result. First, a high positive correlation between the two leads to an equally high but inverse correlation between c_1
and c_2. Thus, biased and relatively meaningless estimates can result, in
spite of a high coefficient of determination. Second, high collinearity
increases the standard errors of the estimated coefficients, thereby pre-
cluding reliable point estimates. It has been shown that many of these collinearity problems can be eliminated by simple first differencing.[2]

Consider equations 4.2 and 4.3 which refer to two successive time
periods, such that

$$Q'_t = A_o + b_1 Y'_t + b_2 T + e_t \qquad (4.2)$$

$$Q'_{t+1} = A_o + b_1 Y'_{t+1} + b_2 (T+1) + e_{t+1} \qquad (4.3)$$

where Q is quantity consumed, Y is income, T is time, and e is a random
error term. Here consumption is a function of income and time and each of
these causal variables are introduced explicitly. Estimation of equations
4.2 and 4.3 separately would yield biased parameter estimates if Y and T
were highly correlated. Let $*Q'_t = Q'_{t+1} - Q'_t$ denote a first difference of
logs. By subtracting equation 4.2 from 4.3 we derive:

$$*Q'_t = b_1 *Y'_t + b_2 + *e_t . \qquad (4.4)$$

In this first difference model the time trend effect has been incorporated

---

[1]For a discussion of autocorrelation see: J. Johnston, _Econometric_
Methods (New York: McGraw-Hill, 1963), chapter vii and the references
cited there.

[2]D. Cochrane and G. H. Orcutt, "Application of Least Squares Regressions to Relationships Containing Auto-Correlated Error Terms," _Journal of the_
American Statistical Association, XXXXIV (1949), 32-61. Also see: Johnston, _op. cit._, chapter viii for a discussion of multicollinearity.

into the constant term, b_2. Therefore, we are able to estimate models such as equation 4.4 and, thereby, circumvent the multicollinearity problem.

Degrees of Freedom and Demand Shifts

Ordinarily, the estimation of a demand function requires time series information on prices, quantities, and other related variables. When one uses such information to estimate the parametric structure of a model one is, implicitly, asserting that those observations have all been generated by the same stochastic mechanism. If such an assertion is valid then a long series of observations is extremely useful. With a greater number of degrees of freedom two desirable benefits accrue; more reliable estimation can be achieved and a larger number of parameters can be accommodated in the model. But, technology does alter over time and the transportation industries exemplify this phenomenon well.[1] Therefore, lengthy time series may or may not be useful depending upon the mechanism generating the observations.

For any type of demand estimation a clear set of observations is a necessary prerequisite. That is, it is desirable to have a set of observations over a time span in which supply shifts have occurred or predominated. Then a clearly delimited demand function can be estimated.[2] Since demand may change over time, it is possible to obtain positive price coefficients during estimation. This, of course, violates one of the a priori demand theory expectations; moreover, it signifies that demand shifts have occurred. This problem can be handled, often, by the inclusion of an income term or a trend variable of some sort, which will account for such shifts and enable the negative demand relationship to be estimated.[3]

Dummy Variables

There has been little discussion in the literature about the dummy variable technique, though it has been frequently utilized.[4] Basically,

[1] Barger, op. cit.

[2] This question is discussed in: Foote, op. cit.

[3] For a good discussion of many estimation problems, especially those relating to time series data, see: F. M. Fisher, A Priori Information and Time Series Analysis: Essays in Economic Theory and Measurement (Amsterdam: North Holland Publishing Company, 1962), chapters i and ii.

[4] In the past few years several expositions of the technique have appeared. See: D. B. Suits, "Use of Dummy Variables in Regression

the technique is a means to enter non-scaled data into regression analysis. It can be used for shift variables such as areas, seasons, or temporal effects; furthermore, it has meaning for the introduction of qualitative variables such as age, sex, and social status. An example will serve to clarify its use.

Suppose we are analyzing the relation between consumption and income by census tracts in a city. Clearly, it is possible to gather numerical information for consumption quantitites and incomes, but the census tract itself is not a properly scaled variable. If we assume that the consumption-income relation, the propensity to consume, is similar among census tracts and only the level of consumption differs, we can estimate such relations independently for each of three census tracts as:

$$C_1 = v_1 + bY$$
$$C_2 = v_2 + bY \tag{4.5}$$
$$C_3 = v_3 + bY$$

where $v_3 > v_2 > v_1$.[1] The solution of the above set of equations requires the estimation of six parameters. Since we are assuming that the propensity to consume, b, is similar in all three census tracts, a more efficient computational procedure would involve pooling the data from all three census tracts to determine a common estimate of b.

We can determine a common slope coefficient by defining a set of three dummy variables, T_1, T_2, T_3, to represent the census tracts analyzed with the property that

$$T_i = 1 \text{ if observation in the } i^{th} \text{ census tract}$$

$$T_i = 0 \text{ otherwise.}$$

One would think the introduction of three such dummy variables leads to a formulation such as

$$C = v_1 + aY + b_{11}T_1 + b_{12}T_2 + b_{13}T_3 \tag{4.6}$$

Equations," _Journal of the American Statistical Association_, LIV (December, 1957), 548-551, and Johnston, _op. cit._, pp. 221-228. For extensive applications of the dummy variable technique, see: G. H. Orcutt _et al._, _Microanalysis of Socioeconomic Systems: A Simulation Study_ (New York: Harper and Row, 1961), and L. R. Klein _et al._, _An Econometric Model of the United Kingdom_ (Oxford: Blackwell, 1961).

[1]Perhaps the census tracts are simply ordered as to personal wealth, such that tract three > tract two > tract one. Under such conditions we might expect $v_3 > v_2 > v_1$.

Unfortunately, equation 4.6 will not suffice since the optimum estimates of v and the b_i are indeterminate. That is, the variance-covariance matrix of equation 4.6 is singular and, therefore, it cannot be inverted.

There are two methods available to circumvent the matrix singularity problem. First, we can set the intercept equal to zero, $v_1 = 0$, which will convert equation 4.6 to

$$C = aY + b_{21}T_1 + b_{22}T_2 = b_{23}T_3 . \qquad (4.7)$$

Note that by setting the intercept equal to zero it has been suppressed and, therefore, it no longer appears in equation 4.7. This procedure allows us to solve equation 4.7 and such solution is determinate for all b_i. Alternatively, we can set one of the dummy coefficients equal to zero, say $b_{13} = 0$, which will convert equation 4.6 to

$$C = v_3 + aY + b_{31}T_1 + b_{32}T_2 . \qquad (4.8)$$

Note that T_3 no longer appears as an explicit independent variable in equation 4.8.

Both formulations, equations 4.7 and 4.8, simply represent differing constraints being placed on the same basic equation, 4.6; therefore, both equations 4.7 and 4.8 will yield the same predictive estimate of the dependent variable, consumption. To indicate that equations 4.7 and 4.8 are simple transformations of one another add $-b_{23}$ to each of the b_{2i} and $+b_{23}$ to the constant term of equation 4.7. The result will be equation 4.8. Thus, $b_{3i} = b_{2i} - b_{23}$.

Equation 4.7 indicates that the dummy coefficients, the b_i, measure the influence of census tracts as deviations from zero because the intercept term has been arbitrarily set equal to zero. On the other hand, the dummy coefficients of equation 4.8 measure the influence of census tract shifts as deviations from the intercept value of tract three, which has been arbitrarily set as the base of comparison.[1]

Previously we stated that the use of dummy variables in problems such as the example discussed are more efficient than the solution of a set of equations such as equation set 4.5. In equation 4.5 six parameters required

---

[1]Additionally, it should be mentioned that the technique allows for interaction effects, such that census tract and income may interact as a joint variable. For discussion of possible types of interaction, see: Orcutt et al., op. cit., and Johnston, op. cit. Once interaction effects are introduced into the regression model, the model becomes indistinguishable from an analysis of covariance. For a discussion of such similarities, see: O. D. Duncan et al., Statistical Geography (Glencoe: The Free Press, 1961), pp. 140-147, and H. Walker and J. Lev, Statistical Inference (New York: Holt, Rinehart, and Winston, 1953), chapter xv.

estimation. In either equation 4.7 and 4.8 only four parameters require estimation. The amount of information derived from either of the latter equations is clearly equivalent to that derived from equation set 4.5. Since
fewer parameters require estimation without a sacrifice in terms of output
information, there has been an efficiency gain in utilizing the dummy variables.[1]

Computing programs that suppress the intercept term, as in equation
4.7, are not too common. But it has been shown that a conventional computing program can be utilized simply by dropping one of the dummy variables
as an explicit independent variable. Furthermore, any number of dummy variable sets can be introduced into a regression function, though the previous
discussion pertained to only one. The only requirement for estimation of
multiple sets is to arbitrarily set one of the coefficients of each set
equal to zero and interpretation proceeds from the base so set.

The Basic Model

In the early part of chapter iii several desirable derived demand
models were presented. Our initial expectation was to pattern a demand model
for freight transportation along the lines of those demand models previously
discussed. Yet, it should be painfully apparent that we are not able to fit
demand functions such as equations 3.1 to 3.5. The requisite input informa-
tion--supplies of individual modes, product output quantities by firm or
groups of firms, and transport consumption by firm or groups of firms--is
not available. Data limitations have forced us to alter our desired demand
model.[2] Furthermore, the existence of only five years of comparable rail-
road-motor carrier data represents a very short time series, irrespective
of the number of parameters to be estimated. In spite of such difficulties
substantive estimation proceeded.

Basically, we attempted to fit a linear demand function of the form:

---

[1] Also, in the event of curvature in the function linear regression
will yield biased parameter estimates. Through the use of dummy variables
we can achieve unbiased parameter estimates, since the regression coefficients of dummy variables conform to any curvature present in the data.

[2] Recently, the Federal Government announced plans to conduct a
Census of Transportation, subsequent to an initial appropriation by Congress.
If additional funds are forthcoming, then a full-scale census will be under-
taken. Hopefully, information will be collected by industry, if not by
firm. Such a census would represent a boon to scholars concerned with the
transportation sector of the economy. Then, data limitations would not be
so restrictive for research, as this study abundantly indicates.

$$\text{Log } Q_i = b_o + b_1 \text{ Log } P_i + b_2 \text{ Log } P_j + \sum_{k=1}^{n} c_k X_k \qquad (i \neq j) \qquad (4.9)$$

where Q_i is transport consumption of mode i, P_i is the price of such consumption, P_j is the price of the alternative mode, and X_i are other related variables.[1] Initially, we attempted to estimate demand by mode for each region and each commodity group. This level of analysis is referred to as the _micro model_.[2] Given nine regions, five major commodity groups, five years of data in each region by commodity group, and two different modes there were, therefore, forty-five demand functions estimated for each mode. Obviously, with only five years of data (five observations) for each function there were severe statistical limitations as to the number of parameters which could be estimated. Yet, estimation proceeded under varying specifications of the basic linear demand model, equation 4.9, such as:

$$
\begin{aligned}
Q_i &= f(P_i) \\
Q_i &= f(P_i, t) \qquad (i \neq j) \qquad (4.10) \\
Q_i &= f(P_i, P_j) \\
Q_i &= f(P_i, P_j, t)
\end{aligned}
$$

where Q is quantity consumed, P is price, and t is a linear time trend.

Since there are only five observations associated with the estimated functions of equation set 4.10, there are few degrees of freedom available for estimation under any of the foregoing model specifications. Dummy variables for time could not be introduced because of the paucity of degrees of freedom. Therefore, a linear time trend was introduced which requires the estimation of only one parameter.

Given the serious statistical limitations of the micro model, our expectations for substantive insights were set low. But, it was hoped that some of the point estimates of price elasticity would be similar between regions. If such similarities were forthcoming then we would have justification for pooling regions. Namely, if region j and region k had similar

---

[1] Price is here defined as revenue per ton. See discussion in _Some Variables_, chapter iv. Furthermore, all prices here and in the modified models were appropriately deflated from nominal prices to real prices. Implicit price deflators for GNP were utilized. See: U. S. Department of Commerce, Office of Business Economics, _Survey of Current Business_ (Washington: Government Printing Office, July, 1961), Table 6, p. 7.

[2] This model most closely resembles the one product-multiple location model of chapter iii. Application here has been extended to five products and nine locations.

point estimates of price elasticity for a given commodity, then there would
be rationale for grouping the two regions. Subsequent to grouping we could
re-estimate demand on the basis of ten observations. With a larger number
of degrees of freedom our estimation procedure would be enhanced and we
would have the opportunity of introducing other variables, such as dummy
vairables, if needed.

In spite of our low threshold of expectation, the results were disappointing. The hoped for similarity of point estimates between regions did
not materialize; thus, we were not able to pool information and gain degrees
of freedom. Clearly, one of the major difficulties associated with estimating equation set 4.10 revolved about the lack of a sufficient number of observations to achieve meaningful resolution. Moreover, the clarity of demand behavior required for successful estimation did not appear to exist.

We next attempted to carry out estimation on alternative levels of
analysis. The meso analysis was applied to aggregation over commodities as
well as aggregation over regions. The former procedure results in estimating transport demand, by mode, for each region; the latter procedure estimates transport demand, by mode, for each commodity group. Both of the
meso models were estimated in terms of the basic linear demand function,
equation 4.9, under the varying specifications of equation set 4.10.

Aggregation over commodities results in estimating demand by region.
Given the five years of information for each of the five commodity groups,
aggregation over commodities results in fitting nine demand functions for
each mode where each function includes twenty-five observations. Since we
now have many more observations than with the micro model, two sets of dummy
variables were included. The first set refers to commodity groups and the
second set to time. Once more our results were of quite variable quality.

By aggregating over regions we applied the meso model to estimating
demand by commodity groups. Given the same five years of data for each
commodity group and region, aggregation over regions results in estimating
demand for each commodity group, by mode, where the estimating function includes forty-five observations. The procedures followed were similar to
those described for commodity aggregation. This time, however, a dummy
variable set for regions was substituted for the commodity set previously
discussed. The results again were rather poor.

Lastly, we aggregated over all commodities and all regions. Demand
estimation proceeded, by mode, where each function included two hundred
twenty-five observations. This we call the macro model. Again, varying
model specifications were estimated, as set forth in equation set 4.10.

This time dummy variables were included for time, region, and commodity group. The results obtained in the micro and two meso models were not substantially improved upon in applying the macro model.

Modified Basic Model

It is evident from the previous discussion that the basic linear demand model adopted for estimation, equation 4.9, needs some modification, if not complete overhaul, for acceptable estimation. At this stage the elasticity of substitution model was introduced, insofar as the basic elasticity model gave such poor and inconclusive results. To reiterate, the elasticity of substitution framework is:

$$Log(Q_i/Q_j) = b_o + b_1 \, Log \, (P_i/P_j) + \sum_{k=1}^{n} c_k Z_k \quad (i \neq j) \quad (4.11)$$

where the relationship links the ratios of quantities consumed and prices.[1] Alternatively, in terms of productive factor inputs, we can define the elasticity of substitution as "the proportionate change in the ratio of the amounts of the factors employed divided by the proportionate change in the ratio of their prices to which it is due."[2] The macro, meso, and micro analyses were then conducted, utilizing the elasticity of substitution framework, under differing sets of model specifications largely similar to those utilized in estimating the basic model. In almost all cases the results were much more heartening than those derived with the basic elasticity model.

The evident disparity of results between the basic model and the modified model, in spite of the same input data, requires some explanation. It appears that the major explanation can be provided through the pricing policies of the regulated transportation agencies. In essence, competitive pricing behavior does not exist in the transport industries.[3] Among the railroads and motor carriers umbrella pricing policies and internal subsidization are quite prevalent.[4] Given a system of umbrella prices for the

---

[1]For the derivation of the elasticity of substitution, b_1, see chapter ii.

[2]J. Robinson, The Economics of Imperfect Competition (London: Macmillan and Company, 1950), p. 256.

[3]See. J. R. Meyer et al., The Economics of Competition in the Transportation Industries (Cambridge: Harvard University Press, 1960). Chapter vii deals with demand characteristics while chapters i and viii concern regulatory practices.

[4]The basis of umbrella pricing is clearly demonstrated in: D. Alexander and L. N. Moses, "Competition under Uneven Regulation," American Economic Review, LIII (May, 1963), 466-474. For examples of internal sub-

two modes, it is exceedingly cumbersome to effectuate price changes with the available regulatory apparatus.[1] Therefore, there is little price fluctuation apparent in the data utilized. Clearly, in the absence of any price variability at all demand estimation for price elasticities would be indeterminate. Thus, it appears that the combination of umbrella pricing, internal subsidization, and little price variability over time account for the difficulties associated with estimating the basic linear demand model. Alternatively, the elasticity of intermodal substitution model of equation 4.11 relates to the relative mix of services produced by the two transport modes. No longer is the estimation emphasis upon the individual prices and their behavior explicitly. Rather the emphasis is upon the relative, not absolute, spread between prices and the market shares of traffic captured by each mode. As such, demand estimation is less restrictive and more meaningful results were obtained.[2]

---

sidization in rate cases coming before the Interstate Commerce Commission, see: E. W. Williams, The Regulation of Rail-Motor Rate Competition (New York: Harper and Brothers, 1958), especially chapter vii.

[1]Williams, op. cit., cites numerous cases appearing before the I.C.C. involving rate adjustments.

[2]Three other matters should be commented upon briefly. First, the logarithmic model is used throughout the subsequent analyses. It was found that the data were not normally distributed and that a logarithmic transformation approximated normality in most cases. Secondly, the regressions were tested for serial correlation by means of a Durbin-Watson statistic. All were non-significant. Third, a discussion of estimation bias due to errors of measurement is not particularly germane to this study. For such a discussion, see: G. H. Orcutt, "Measurement of Price Elasticities in International Trade," Review of Economics and Statistics, XXXII (May, 1950), 117-132; and for a more recent but related discussion, see: M. C. Kemp, "Errors of Measurement and Bias in Estimates of Import Demand Parameters," Economic Record, XXXVIII (September, 1962), 369-373.

CHAPTER V

MACRO ANALYSIS

The macro model, outlined in chapter iv, attempts to estimate total
transportation demand by mode for the continental United States. Given our
data source materials[1] it is possible to view such a model as the grouping
of all commodity groups into a time series analysis over a five-year horizon.
Such an aggregation model would be unduly restrictive with few degrees of
freedom available for estimation purposes. That is, regional and commodity
demand effects would be excluded from such a research design. We do not
expect, a priori, that all goods movement operates within a unitary market
of national dimension. Rather, the existence of several or many markets prevail, where such market structures are distinguished either spatially or by
types of commodities handled. We have, accordingly, aggregated our data
from the individual commodity and region basis to a national series for all
commodities over all regions. This type of aggregation will permit the inclusion of shift variables for estimation purposes.

The Basic Macro Model

Initially, the basic model of equation 4.9 was applied to the nation
as a single observational unit within which only price effects on transport
demand were analyzed. Separate functions for motor carrier and railroad
demands were estimated, such as

$$\text{Log } Q_m = a_m + b_{mm} \text{ Log } P_m + b_{mr} \text{ Log } P_r \qquad (5.1)$$

and

$$\text{Log } Q_r = a_r + b_{rm} \text{ Log } P_m + b_{rr} \text{ Log } P_r, \qquad (5.2)$$

where the subscripts m and r refer to motor carriers and railroads respectively.[2] In order to estimate 5.1 and 5.2 for the nation as a unit, we

---

[1] Data sources were presented in chapter iii.

[2] There are many examples of demand studies following this type of
format. Some recent examples are: A. P. Koutsoyannis, "Demand Functions
for Tobacco," The Manchester School of Economic and Social Studies, XXXI
(January, 1963), 1-19, and G. W. Taylor, "Meat Consumption in Australia,"
The Economic Record, XXXIX (March, 1963), 81-87. Also, see G. Tintner,
Econometrics (New York: John Wiley, 1952), for many examples of similar
types of demand studies.

aggregated our data over all regions, commodities, and years. Given nine regions, five commodity groups, and five years of information, there are 9 x 5 x 5 = 225 observations available.[1] The results of estimating equations 5.1 and 5.2 are presented in Table 1.

TABLE 1

ESTIMATES OF EQUATIONS 5.1 AND 5.2

	Coeffi-cient	Estimate	Standard Error	Coeffi-cient	Estimate	Standard Error
Intercept	a_m	6.4499		a_r	6.5429	
Prices						
P_m	b_{mm}	-2.0230**	.1966	b_{rm}	- .9790**	.1788
P_r	b_{mr}	1.5538**	.1679	b_{rr}	- .7226**	.1528
	R^2	.3587		R^2	.3437	

**Significant at .01 level.

Though all the coefficients of 5.1 and 5.2 are statistically significant the over-all fit, for both functions, does not appear to be particularly good. Motor carrier demand appears to be highly price elastic (-2.0230) with railroad service representing an important substitute (1.5538). On the other hand, railroad demand appears to be mildly price inelastic (-.7226) with motor carriers representing an important complementary service (-.9790). These relationships display, obviously a lack of symmetry in the cross price elasticities. Whereas, railroad services represent a substitutable good for motor carrier demands motor carrier services are complementary goods for railroad demands.

Assume these two modes are the only means of transporting commodities. Then we would expect symmetric cross effects in signs because the two modes would be the only effective substitutes for one another.[2] Of course, there are other transport modes available for commodity flows and, therefore, there are system leakages; but, other modes carry a smaller frac-

---

[1]The regions utilized are shown in Figure 2, chapter iii. Commodity groups and the availability of annual data were described in chapter iii, also.

[2]A discussion of cross effect relations under sutstitution was given in chapter ii.

tion of total goods flows, except for petroleum pipelines.[1] Thus, most goods will be carried by either of the modes under analysis and we should expect symmetry or near symmetry in the cross price effects. The magnitudes and the signs of the cross price effects apparent in Table 1 do not support our a priori concepts about the symmetry of demand patterns.

In terms of own price elasticities (b_{mm} and b_{rr}) we do not expect such a large dispartiy between the estimates obtained. Motor carrier demand appears to be unusually elastic together with effective railroad substitution. Recent railroad experience manifests the loss of certain types of traffic with concomitant capture on the part of motor carriers.[2] But our estimated price elasticity (-.7226) is somewhat inelastic, together with a negative sign associated with the motor carrier cross effect. Under these conditions there should be little reason for significant traffic losses on the part of the railroads nor the existence of significant competition between the modes. These parameter estimates, equations 5.1 and 5.2, are perplexing, indeed.

Naturally, one cannot help but inquire if there has been any bias introduced in the estimation of the parameters represented in Table 1. It seems reasonable to attribute the strange behavior of the elasticity estimates to our aggregation process. If comparative advantage exists, as alleged, then price elasticities should vary either according to commodity markets or regional markets.[3] Grouping all commodities together in one demand function will tend to bias the results toward the large tonnage observations, those represented by the bulk commodity flows. This is precisely the traffic category that the railroads have been most successful in retaining. Low valued bulk commodities should generate elastic point estimates. Yet, this explanation implies that motor carrier demand should not be very elastic. Our estimates indicate otherwise. Because of the many questions raised in the resolution of 5.1 and 5.2, the theoretical meaning and interpretation of the estimated parameters, and the relatively poor explanatory power of the model, we place little credence in the parameter estimates of Table 1.

---

[1] Of all transportation modes, pipelines accounted for 16-18 per cent of total intercity goods flow over the interval 1955-1960. See: U.S. Interstate Commerce Commission, Bureau of Transport Economics and Statistics, Intercity Ton-Miles 1939-1959, op. cit., Table 1.

[2] Ibid.

[3] Meyer et al., op. cit., pp. 146-162, on competition between modes for types of commodities. On regional and/or commodity markets, see chapter vii as well.

The Basic Model--Augmented

If transportation demand is composed of sub-national markets, both spatially and in terms of commodity types, then shift variables ought to be included in our estimation procedure to account for such differential effects. Given our doubts about the extent and structure of the transportation market and/or markets together with the perplexing estimates of equations 5.1 and 5.2, we chose to investigate an alternative specification of the basic model. This time we shall estimate transport demand by mode but shift variables for region, commodity and year will be introduced. Hopefully, the variability of total transport demand will be illuminated by considering such shift effects together with pricing effects, simultaneously. Therefore, we estimated

$$\text{Log } Q_m = a_m + b_{mm} \text{ Log } P_m + b_{mr} \text{ Log } P_r + \sum_{i=2}^{9} c_{mi} R_i + \sum_{j=2}^{5} d_{mj} T_j + \sum_{k=2}^{5} f_{mk} Z_k \qquad (5.3)$$

and

$$\text{Log } Q_r = a_r + b_{rm} \text{ Log } P_m + b_{rr} \text{ Log } P_r + \sum_{i=2}^{9} c_{ri} R_i + \sum_{j=2}^{5} d_{rj} T_j + \sum_{k=2}^{5} f_{rk} Z_k \qquad (5.4)$$

where the subscripts m and r refer to motor carriers and railroads.[1] The R_i, T_j, and Z_k are dummy variable sets for region, year, and commodity group, where

$$R_i = \begin{cases} 1 & \text{if observation in } i^{th} \text{ region} \\ 0 & \text{otherwise} \end{cases}$$

$$T_j = \begin{cases} 1 & \text{if observation } j^{th} \text{ year} \\ 0 & \text{otherwise} \end{cases}$$

$$Z_k = \begin{cases} 1 & \text{if observation is } k^{th} \text{ commodity group} \\ 0 & \text{otherwise} \end{cases}$$

In order to permit estimation of equations 5.3 and 5.4 one

---

[1]The following coding is used throughout the remainder of this study:

Regions	Years	Commodities
R_1 = Southern	T_1 = 1956	Z_1 = Manufactures and misc.
R_2 = Middle Atlantic	T_2 = 1957	Z_2 = Products of forests
R_3 = New England	T_3 = 1958	Z_3 = Products of mines
R_4 = Central	T_4 = 1959	Z_4 = Animals and products
R_5 = Northwest	T_5 = 1960	Z_5 = Products of agriculture
R_6 = Midwest		
R_7 = Southwest		
R_8 = Rocky Mountain		
R_9 = Pacific		

These classifications were thoroughly discussed in chapter iii.

dummy variable from each set needs to be omitted.[1] Arbitrarily, it was decided to drop variables R_1, T_1, and Z_1, which represent the Southern Region,
the year 1956, and Manufactures.[2] Thus, the standard intercepts of 5.3 and
5.4 refer to the specific demand combination composed of the Southern Region,
the year 1956, and Manufacturers. All other shift variables estimated
utilize the omitted members as a base from which deviations are measured.[3]
The results of estimating equations 5.3 and 5.4 are presented in Table 2.

Clearly, the over-all fit of equations 5.3 and 5.4 is substantially
better than was the case with 5.1 and 5.2 and this alone is encouraging.
All of the price elasticities have been greatly reduced in absolute value
from the previous case. Moreover, the striking asymmetry of cross price
effects noted previously is no longer so marked, though still present.
Table 2 indicates that railroad services are substitutes for motor carrier
demand and these parameter estimates (5.3) are statistically significant.
In terms of railroad demand (5.4) the motor carrier cross price effect still
indicates that it is a complementary good, but neither of these estimates
is significant now. With regard to the shift variables, the commodity and
region variables seem to be highly significant and the time variables appear
non-significant. Most of the additional explanatory power of equations 5.3
and 5.4 is attributable to the highly significant commodity shift variable
set; some additional explanation is provided by the regional variable set.
The lack of significance of the time variable set implies little additional
explanation above that provided by pricing effects alone.

The elasticity estimates of Table 1 were discounted because of their
asymmetric signs and the over-all poor fit of the model, in spite of statistically significant coefficient estimates. In the present case (Table 2)
the over-all fit of the equations is good, but note the parameter estimates.
Here again, the parameter estimates for motor carrier demand are statistically significant. If motor carriers and railroads are substitutes then
the signs of the elasticities are correct. Even the magnitude of the motor

---

[1]Refer to discussion of dummy variable estimation in chapter iv
about the necessity of omitting one member of each dummy variable set.

[2]Since our data cover the years 1956-1960, dropping T_1 implies
measuring all other years relative to 1956 as a base. The regional and
commodity sets present no simple analogous pattern. The southern region
and manufactures were arbitrary choices. R_1, T_1, and Z_1 will be the omitted
variables in all subsequent analyses.

[3]For an example of a study using several dummy variable sets as
equations 5.3 and 5.4, see: M. Kurz and A. S. Manne, "Engineering Estimates of Capital-Labor Substitution in Metal Machining," American Economic
Review, LIII (September, 1963), 662-679.

TABLE 2

ESTIMATES OF EQUATIONS 5.3 AND 5.4

	Coefficient	Estimate	Standard Error	Coefficient	Estimate	Standard Error
Intercept	a_m	8.4694		a_r	6.1614	
Prices						
P_m	b_{mm}	-1.6325**	.1104	b_{rm}	- .3287	.1931
P_r	b_{mr}	.5132**	.1110	b_{rr}	- .0142	.1942
Regions						
R_2	c_{m2}	- .3438**	.0603	c_{r2}	- .2661*	.1056
R_3	c_{m3}	- .9719**	.0608	c_{r3}	-1.0817**	.1064
R_4	c_{m4}	.0087	.0590	c_{r4}	.0293	.1033
R_5	c_{m5}	- .6803**	.0598	c_{r5}	- .2369*	.1048
R_6	c_{m6}	- .4003**	.0595	c_{r6}	- .3087**	.1041
R_7	c_{m7}	- .2669**	.0595	c_{r7}	- .1436	.1041
R_8	c_{m8}	- .4367**	.0648	c_{r8}	- .3359**	.1134
R_9	c_{m9}	- .4005**	.0740	c_{r9}	- .3448**	.1296
Years						
T_2	d_{m2}	.0274	.0440	d_{r2}	- .0403	.0770
T_3	d_{m3}	.0211	.0440	d_{r3}	- .0876	.0770
T_4	d_{m4}	.1093*	.0440	d_{r4}	- .0845	.0770
T_5	d_{m5}	.1383**	.0442	d_{r5}	- .0924	.0773
Commodities						
Z_2	f_{m2}	-1.9182**	.0555	f_{r2}	-.7986**	.0971
Z_3	f_{m3}	-1.6462**	.0931	f_{r3}	.0059	.1629
Z_4	f_{m4}	-1.1119**	.0600	f_{r4}	-1.4714**	.1050
Z_5	f_{m5}	-1.2984**	.0488	f_{r5}	- .3822**	.0855
	R^2	.9458		R^2	.7951	

*Significant at .05 level.

**Significant at .01 level.

carrier estimates seem likely. That is, the own price elasticity (-1.6325) indicates that motor carrier services are price responsive and this accords with a competitive market. The positive sign for the railroad cross effect further supports the notion of market competition. On the other hand, the railroad demand function appears to yield poor estimates in magnitude and

sign; both of the elasticities are non-significant, too. The almost perfect price inelasticity of railroad demand coupled with a large standard error
and a negative cross effect leads to a very different conclusion than for the
motor carriers. High inelasticity implies little price sensitivity and a
negative cross effect implies complementarity not substitution. Conclusions
reached from Table 2 are quite disparate and promote scepticism. Motor carrier demand estimates appear likely, but the railroad demand estimates are
highly suspect and lack theoretical support. This is an uncomfortable conclusion.

One last alternative is available for estimating the basic linear
model on a national aggregative basis. It is clear from Table 2 that the
increased explanatory power of equations 5.3 and 5.4 above that provided by
5.1 and 5.2 is primarily attributable to the commodity shift variables. In
order to understand more fully the simultaneous effects of a large set of
variables (5.3 and 5.4) as well as to eliminate redundancies in the system,
we estimated pricing effects with one shift variable set at a time. Obviously, the commodity variable set provided the greatest additional explanatory power in equations 5.3 and 5.4; therefore, transport demand by
mode was estimated as a function of prices and commodities. The demand
functions are:

$$\text{Log } Q_m = a_m + b_{mm} \text{ Log } P_m + b_{mr} \text{ Log } P_r + \sum_{k=2}^{5} f_{mk} Z_k \tag{5.5}$$

and

$$\text{Log } Q_r = a_r + b_{rm} \text{ Log } P_m + b_{rr} \text{ Log } P_r + \sum_{k=2}^{5} f_{rk} Z_k \tag{5.6}$$

where m and r are motor carriers and railroads. Results of this estimation
are included in Table 3.

A comparison of Tables 1, 2, and 3 will be most instructive. Recall that the first table is the macro model with price effects alone; the
second table includes region, time, and commodity variables as well as price
effects; the last table includes pricing effects and a set of commodity shift
variables. Note that the fit of 5.5 and 5.6, Table 3, is quite good. Clearly
most of the additional explanation of the shift variables in Table 2 as contrasted with Tabe 1 is attributable to the commodity variable set, exemplified by Table 3. Also, motor carrier price elasticity of Table 3
(-1.3762) is the lowest, in absolute value, of the three estimates; own
price elasticity is highly significant and cross price elasticity is now
non-significant. In fact, the combination of a very low cross elasticity
estimate and its large standard error indicates that perhaps the true estimate is quite close to zero. This cross elasticity, its non-significance,

TABLE 3

ESTIMATES OF EQUATIONS 5.5 AND 5.6

	Coefficient	Estimate	Standard Error	Coefficient	Estimate	Standard Error
Intercept	a_m	8.1933		a_r	5.8811	
Prices						
P_m	b_{mm}	-1.3762**	.1446	b_{rm}	- .0692	.1907
P_r	b_{mr}	.2138	.1488	b_{rr}	- .3432	.1962
Commodities						
z_2	f_{m2}	-2.0373**	.0860	f_{r2}	- .9261**	.1134
z_3	f_{m3}	-1.7356**	.1372	f_{r3}	- .1006	.1809
z_4	f_{m4}	-1.1112**	.0941	f_{r4}	-1.4646**	.1240
z_5	f_{m5}	-1.3732**	.0792	f_{r5}	- .4609**	.1044
	R^2	.8347		R^2	.6450	

*Significant at .05 level.

**Significant at .01 level.

and its very small value are all characteristics which differ from our previous estimates of the cross elasticity with respect to motor carrier demand.

On the other hand, the railroad price elasticity (-.3432) is larger in Table 3 than in Table 2 though it is non-significant and still highly inelastic. More important, however, is the exceedingly small estimate of the cross elasticity with respect to railroad demand (-.0692) and its very large standard error. It is just as likely that the sign of the cross effect is positive as it is negative. This measure of uncertainty is somewhat disturbing since it does not allow one to give a reliable point estimate for the cross effect. Yet it is somewhat satisfying that our a priori expectations of substitutable relations between modes is now partly defendable. At least, the marked asymmetry of cross effects in Tables 1 and 2 has been replaced by a more acceptable estimate, which may or may not represent a substitutable service. Notice that the motor carrier own price elasticity is now somewhat elastic, though slightly. Conversely, the railroad own price elasticity is highly inelastic. If the railroads do maintain a comparative advantage for bulk shipments then we should expect some elasticity in the national model, but the large inelasticity estimate seems overly large. It indicates that commodities carried by the railroads are insensitive to price changes. This is the exact opposite conclusion we would expect. Lastly, all the commodity shift parameters are significant, with one exception.

In our analysis of three specifications of the macro model it has become apparent that pricing effects alone will not suffice for explaining national transportation demand, by mode, if all commodities are grouped into a total demand function as 5.1 and 5.2. The addition of shift variable sets, as 5.3 and 5.4, improves the over-all explanatory and predictive power of the model, but it yields some parameter estimates which have little theoretical support. The last model specification, 5.5 and 5.6, operates rather well for motor carriers both in terms of explanatory power and meaningful point estimates. It appears that the bias of large bulk shipments, which should be elastic, is not forthcoming. The extremely large inelastic railroad estimates obtained together with complementary cross effects defy sound interpretation. Therefore, we are not wholly content with our results.

Modified Macro Model

Since many questions about the meaning of the basic macro model estimates remain, we decided to utilize the elasticity of substitution concept. Hopefully, more meaningful results would be forthcoming under the modified macro model. Recourse to the modified basic model, such as equation 4.11, was adopted when the basic linear model did not perform as was anticipated. Recall from chapter iv that there is a slightly different interpretation of elasticity of substitution estimates than the price elasticities of the basic model. The two concepts are intimately related, though.[1]

The elasticity of substitution estimates that we will present refer to the relative mix of the two transport modes under analysis and their demands. Relative prices between these two substitutable modes serve to allocate consumptive choices and, therefore, the market shares of traffic captured by each mode. Our recourse to the modified macro model does not represent a theoretical retreat. Rather, it is an alternative demand model specification which may operate more effectively than the basic macro model in obtaining meaningful elasticity estimates.

Our method of approach or sequence of analysis is similar to the

---

[1]For the theoretical relationships see chapter ii, Elasticity of Substitution.

basic model. First, we estimate demand under a simple price-quantity relationship. Then we add sets of shift variables to examine their simultaneous effects. Lastly, we re-examine only those shift variable sets which
significantly aid meaningful estimation. Since this sequence of analysis
replicates the basic macro model strategy the estimates obtained can be
compared quite readily.

The process of data aggregation for national transport demand estimation was discussed in the previous section. Input data used in that
section were reorganized into the following elasticity of substitution
framework:

$$\text{Log} \ (Q_m/Q_r) = a + b \ \text{Log} \ (P_m/P_r) \tag{5.7}$$

where the subscripts m and r refer to motor carriers and railroads, as before. Clearly, the causality of the model operates from relative rather
than absolute prices to relative quantities or market shares of freight
capture. The results of estimating 5.7 are presented in Table 4.[1]

TABLE 4

ESTIMATES OF EQUATION 5.7

	Coefficient	Estimate	Standard Error
Intercept	a	1.0975	
Price Variable			
Log (P_m/P_r)	b	-1.8716**	.1449
Coefficient of Deter- mination	R^2	.4277	

**Significant at .01 level.

The goodness of fit indicated in Table 4 is rather similar to
Table 1--mediocre. Apparently, relative prices alone leave much variability in market shares unaccounted. This result confirms our earlier es-

[1]See the following recent articles which utilize the elasticity
of substitution concept: Zelder, op. cit.; H. Demsetz, "The Effect of
Consumer Experience on Brand Loyalty and the Structure of Market Demand,"
Econometrica, XXX (January, 1962), 22-33; I. Horowitz, "An Econometric
Analysis of Supply and Demand in the Synthetic Rubber Industry," Inter-
national Economic Review, IV (September, 1963), 325-345; and M. G. Reid,
"Consumer Response to the Relative Price of Store Versus Delivered Milk,"
The Journal of Political Economy, LXXI (April, 1963), 180-186.

timates. Yet, the elasticity of substitution estimate is highly significant
and rather similar to the price elasticity for motor carrier demand in Table
1. Our doubts about the magnitude of that estimate in Table 1 can be reiter-
ated in the present case as well. Namely, the elasticity estimate for equation 5.7 seems too large, though the sign is in the right direction. This
estimate (-1.8716) indicates that these two modes are very effective substitutes for one another; otherwise, a much smaller estimate would have been
obtained. That is, given a small percentage change in relative prices (say,
1%) there will result a highly elastic reaction in relative consumption and,
therefore, market share composition. Our analysis of Table 1 yielded a
similar result for motor carrier demand (highly elastic), but a rather
different result for railroad demand (rather inelastic). In the present
instance we are combining the previous two relations, equations 5.1 and
5.2, into one function. There seems little reason to expect the motor
carrier component to so completely dominate the combined relationship.
Given our theoretical doubts as well as the large amount of unexplained
variability in equation 5.7, we place little stock in the results of
Table 4.

Modified Macro Model--Augmented

As was the case in the basic macro model, there is strong reason
to believe that aggregate national transport demand cannot be meaningfully
estimated in terms of grouping all commodities and areas. Shift variable
sets need to be introduced to represent regions, years, and commodities.
Seemingly, several markets are being analyzed simultaneously in a national
demand function as 5.7 where the results of the several markets are completely homogenized. There is strong reason to believe that regional and
commodity markets exist in transportation. These types of questions can only
be effectively analyzed and their influences estimated in a national demand
model if shift variables are explicitly introduced. Equation 5.8 is an
elasticity of substitution model which includes dummy variable sets for regions, years and commodities. Symbolically, it is:

$$\text{Log } (Q_m/Q_r) = a + b \text{ Log}(P_m/P_r) + \sum_{i=2}^{9} c_i R_i + \sum_{j=2}^{5} d_j T_j + \sum_{k=2}^{5} f_k Z_k \qquad (5.8)$$

where the R_i, T_j, and Z_k are dichotomous variables for regions, years, and
commodities.[1] The results of fitting equation 5.8 are displayed in Table 5.

---

[1]The coding of the dummy variables follows the system outlined on
page 45, footnote 1.

TABLE 5

ESTIMATES OF EQUATION 5.8

	Coefficient	Estimate	Standard Error
Intercept	a	1.5359	
Price Variable			
Log (P_m/P_r)	b	$-$ .9177**	.1269
Regions			
R_2	c_2	$-$ .0378	.0983
R_3	c_3	.1163	.0999
R_4	c_4	$-$ .0231	.0971
R_5	c_5	$-$ .4168**	.0980
R_6	c_6	$-$ .1248	.0972
R_7	c_7	$-$ .0949	.0973
R_8	c_8	$-$ .2220*	.0984
R_9	c_9	$-$ .0463	.1217
Years			
T_2	d_2	.0626	.0723
T_3	d_3	.1089	.0724
T_4	d_4	.2003**	.0723
T_5	d_5	.2491**	.0724
Commodities			
Z_2	f_2	-1.0723**	.0898
Z_3	f_3	-1.2611**	.0787
Z_4	f_4	.1603*	.0725
Z_5	f_5	$-$ .9301**	.0802
Coefficient of Determination	R^2	.8450	

*Significant at .05 level.

**Significant at .01 level.

The first characteristic of 5.8 to note is the greatly improved predictive power of the model. This result parallels our experience in Table 2. Secondly, the elasticity of substitution estimate has been drastically reduced from equation 5.7 and now appears to approximate unitary price elasticity. This implies near competitive behavior. Note the statistical sig-

nificance of the elasticity parameter and the commodity estimates. Once
again, the commodity estimates appear to provide most of the explanatory
power of the model beyond simple price effects. The regional shift variables are almost all non-significant and only one-half of the time variables are significant. Also, notice the marked non-linearity evidenced
by the time coefficient estimates.

Because of our previous experience with redundant variables and
their influences, it was decided to re-estimate the elasticity of substitution parameter with only those shift variables which appear to provide
meaningful resolution for our model. Therefore, an alternative specification was attempted where price and commodity variables are included,
such as

$$\text{Log } (Q_m/Q_r) = a + b \text{ Log } (P_m/P_r) + \sum_{k=2}^{5} f_k Z_k \qquad (5.9)$$

The results of 5.9 are displayed in Table 6.

TABLE 6

ESTIMATES OF EQUATION 5.9

	Coefficient	Estimate	Standard Error
Intercept	a	1.5649	
Price Variable			
Log (P_m/P_r)	b	- .9413**	.1011
Commodities			
Z_2	f_2	-1.0624**	.0897
Z_3	f_3	-1.2554**	.0828
Z_4	f_4	.1611*	.0792
Z_5	f_5	- .9237**	.0837
Coefficient of Determination	R^2	.8040	

*Significant at .05 level.
**Significant at .01 level.

Estimation of equation 5.9 indicates that the commodity shift variables provide most of the explanatory power of 5.8, as suspected. Here
they have been estimated free of the redundancy effects apparent in equation 5.8. All coefficients of 5.9 are significant and the elasticity

estimates of 5.8 and 5.9 are nearly identical. The elasticity estimates seem to have stabilized, though at a much smaller value than that indicated in Table 4. Furthermore, the standard intercepts for 5.8 and 5.9 are most similar. This combination of confirmatory evidence is rewarding.

The standard intercept of Table 6 refers to the level of demand as reflected by Z_1, manufactures. All other commodity shift variables are measured from it as a datum. Our elasticity of substitution formulation indicates that demand elasticity of -.9413 represents an over-all type of elasticity average for all commodities, but the level of demand alters according to specific commodity groups. Note that three of the commodity groups (products of forests, products of mines, and products of agriculture) have negative signs associated with their estimates and, therefore, represent lower levels of demand than do manufactures. Animals and products, Z_4, displays a higher level of aggregate demand than does manufactures.

Why does the present price elasticity seem plausible? Recall from chapter ii that the ordinary law of demand postulates an inverse relation between quantity of a good consumed and its price. The present formulation, the elasticity of substitution approach, says that demand and market shares will be a function of relative prices of two substitutable transport modes. Our estimate (-.9413) says that a 10% rise in the price ratio will effectuate a less than proportionate decrease in the consumption ratio, though only slightly less (9.4%). Obviously, the price ratio can increase by 10% if either the numerator increases or the denominator decreases or some combination of the two.

In the first instance assume a price rise in P_m such that the ratio Log (P_m/P_r) increases by 10%. Under normal demand conditions we would, therefore, expect motor carrier consumption to decrease. This decrease would be countered by a consumption shift out of motor carriers and into railroad services if the two modes are substitutable and the level of output is to be maintained. Railroad consumption would increase then. Further, assume that the motor carrier price rise is the only change in the system. Then motor carrier consumption will decrease until the quantity ratio is approximately 10% less than before the price alteration.

We could just as easily have traced the effects through the system resulting from a decrease in P_r which would have caused a 10% alteration in Log (P_m/P_r). Under this condition the price decrease would have precipitated an increase in railroad consumption or Q_r would increase. It would increase until the ratio Log (Q_m/Q_r) was 9.4% less than before the price change. Clearly, the present result is identical to the previous result and serves to indicate that the consumption reaction operates irrespective of the source of the price change. Lastly, the price ratio could increase or decrease due to a combination of price alterations in the individual modes.[1] Here again, the result would have been the same or the generation of a price elasticity of -.9413. The elasticity of substitution, therefore, depends upon relative changes alone. This, of course, has particular pertinence to the transportation industries where umbrella pricing is common and the price spread between mode services is the crucial issue, not the absolute prices.

TABLE 7

COMMODITY DEMAND FUNCTIONS--MACRO ANALYSIS

Z_1 - Manufacture and Misc. $\text{Log } (Q_m/Q_r) = 1.5649 - .9413 \text{ Log } (P_m/P_r)$

Z_2 - Products of Forests $\text{Log } (Q_m/Q_r) = .5025 - .9413 \text{ Log } (P_m/P_r)$

Z_3 - Products of Mines $\text{Log } (Q_m/Q_r) = .3095 - .9413 \text{ Log } (P_m/P_r)$

Z_4 - Animals and Products $\text{Log } (Q_m/Q_r) = 1.7267 - .9413 \text{ Log } (P_m/P_r)$

Z_5 - Products of Agriculture $\text{Log } (Q_m/Q_r) = .6412 - .9413 \text{ Log } (P_m/P_r)$

Table 7 presents the results of equation 5.9 reorganized into separate demand functions by commodity group. Of course, our estimation process yields an average or central tendency type of price elasticity. Therefore, b = -.9413 appears as the elasticity of substitution in all five functions. On the other hand, note the wide variation in the effective level of demand, from .3095 to 1.7267, resulting from the differential behavior of commodity groups. Due to this demand level fluctuation there is ample reason to suggest that transportation demand may vary according to commodities handled. Also, each commodity set may represent a different transportation market with its own set of structural characteristics. Furthermore, there was evidence (Tables 2 and 5) to suggest that transport demand may be composed of dissimilar regional markets, though this evidence was not as well founded as the commodity case. If these two sets of sub-national markets do, in fact, prevail then maybe different price elasticities pertain to them, though they be masked in the averaging effect of the macro model. We, therefore, intend to investigate questions associated with sub-national markets, both by region and commodity.

[1] This last possibility is the most likely market outcome, of course.

CHAPTER VI

MESO ANALYSIS BY COMMODITIES

Our analysis of total national demand presented in chapter v resulted in estimates of price elasticities and insights about market organization. The analysis and estimates were of a substantive nature and ac-
corded well with some widely held views about the organization of the transportation industry. Nevertheless, a certain amount of transportation demand
was left unexplained. Some evidence was presented to indicate that perhaps
such explanation may be provided by analyzing sub-national markets. Apparently a sufficient amount of national demand variation may better be under-
stood through the analysis of commodity markets or regional markets. The
former case is being examined in this chapter.

A research strategy was advanced in the macro analysis and that
research design will be followed in the present chapter as well. So far,
the research design appears meaningful and the similarities of analysis
for national demand and commodity demand will, therefore, enhance compari-
sons.

The Basic Model

There appears to be some evidence to indicate that transportation
demand variability may partly be attributable to differential behavior of
the several types of commodities handled.[1] Therefore, we have rearranged
our input data so that transport demand may be estimated by separate commodity groups. Recall that we have available data on nine regions, five
commodity groups, and five years of observations or a total of two hundred
twenty-five observations. These have been re-ordered into separate sets
for each commodity category such that demand for each commodity group is
based upon forty-five observations.

Our first commodity model attempts to determine the effects of
pricing behavior and it is analogous to the basic model or equation 4.9.
Two demand functions are formulated, one for each transport mode, such
that

---

[1]See Table 7, chapter v, and the associated discussion presented
there.

$$\text{Log } Q_m = a_m + b_{mm} \text{ Log } P_m + b_{mr} \text{ Log } P_r \tag{6.1}$$

and

$$\text{Log } Q_r = a_r + b_{rm} \text{ Log } P_m + b_{rr} \text{ Log } P_r \tag{6.2}$$

where m and r pertain to motor carriers and railroads. Estimates of equations 6.1 and 6.2 are presented in Tables 8 and 9; the former table pertains to motor carrier demands (6.1) and the latter table to railroad demands (6.2).

Less than one-half of the parameter estimates of Tables 8 and 9 are significant. Two estimates of own price elasticity are positive, motor carrier demand for manufactures (.3783) and railroad demand for animals (1.4057). Such a result deviates from expected ordinary demand behavior and is, therefore, suspect. Only one of the fitted functions displays a reasonable amount of explanation, motor carrier demand for mine products. Since the goodness of fit is so poor for nine out of the ten functions there is little reason to place much confidence in the estimates obtained, though some of them are statistically significant. Basically, the results of equations 6.1 and 6.2 indicate that little explanation is provided for transportation consumption according to commodity groups as a result of pricing behavior alone.

Because of the poor estimates obtained from 6.1 and 6.2 the basic model may again be augmented by the addition of shift variable sets for regional and temporal variations. In order to augment the basic model we merely add two sets of dummy variables and re-estimate demand separately for each mode, where each estimated function pertains to one commodity group. Therefore, five functions are fitted for each mode such that

$$\text{Log } Q_m = a_m + b_{mm} \text{ Log } P_m + b_{mr} \text{ Log } P_r + \sum_{i=2}^{9} c_{mi} R_i + \sum_{j=2}^{5} d_{mj} T_j \tag{6.3}$$

and

$$\text{Log } Q_r = a_r + b_{rm} \text{ Log } P_m + b_{rr} \text{ Log } P_r + \sum_{i=2}^{9} c_{ri} R_i + \sum_{j=2}^{5} d_{rj} T_j \tag{6.4}$$

where the R_i are the regions and the T_j are years. Estimates of equations 6.3 and 6.4 are provided in Tables 10 and 11, respectively.

A comparison of Tables 8 and 9 with Tables 10 and 11 serves to indicate the appreciable improvement obtained in explanation. In fact, all functions have R^2 equal to or greater than .98 and more than one-half of all estimated parameters in Tables 10 and 11 have significant coefficients. Such a degree of explanation does not necessarily imply an equally high degree of meaningfulness in the estimates obtained. Of the twenty price variables in the two tables only six display significant parameter estimates

TABLE 8

ESTIMATES OF EQUATION 6.1

	Manufac-tures	Forests	Mines	Animals	Agricul-ture
Intercept					
a_m	8.1284	7.1805	6.7830	5.5593	6.7062
Price Variables					
b_{mm}	.3783	-2.0594**	-2.2541**	-.3710	-1.2142**
	(.5290)	(.2902)	(.2733)	(.2464)	(.3690)
b_{mr}	1.4166	-.1270	.7266	.4231	.1360
	(.7866)	(.1942)	(.4110)	(.3272)	(.3386)
Coefficient of Determination					
R^2	.0984	.5495	.7127	.0686	.2999

**Significant at .01 level.

TABLE 9

ESTIMATES OF EQUATION 6.2

	Manufac-tures	Forests	Mines	Animals	Agricul-ture
Intercept					
a_r	6.7134	6.8617	6.0905	1.8108	7.1077
Price Variables					
b_{rr}	-2.1865**	-.1400	-.9545	1.4057**	-1.5771**
	(.7765)	(.2918)	(.7094)	(.3864)	(.3772)
b_{rm}	.9889	-1.8929**	-.1907	.2631	-.5827
	(.5222)	(.4359)	(.4717)	(.2910)	(.4110)
Coefficient of Determination					
R^2	.2597	.3148	.0422	.2905	.3075

**Significant at .01 level.

TABLE 10

ESTIMATES OF EQUATION 6.3

	Manufac-tures	Forests	Mines	Animals	Agricul-ture
Intercept					
a_m	8.0491	6.7319	6.5744	5.2889	6.7837
Price Variables					
b_{mm}	-.7152**	-1.3480**	-1.1828**	-.1564	-.7329
	(.1665)	(.2576)	(.1391)	(.2516)	(.2816)
b_{mr}	-.1662	-.1394	.0358	.5636	-.3474
	(.5395)	(.4128)	(.4395)	(.3315)	(.4251)
Regions					
c_{m2}	.1717**	-.3678*	-.0583	.0542	-.4680**
	(.0353)	(.1570)	(.0585)	(.1369)	(.0894)
c_{m3}	-.5703**	-.7659**	-.9783**	-.6913**	-.7673**
	(.0650)	(.0690)	(.0547)	(.0922)	(.1251)
c_{m4}	.4372**	-.1238	.0286	.1719**	-.4250**
	(.0481)	(.0988)	(.0814)	(.0563)	(.1052)
c_{m5}	-.4607**	-.5845**	-.8268**	-.1304	-.6224**
	(.0760)	(.1051)	(.1722)	(.1322)	(.0766)
c_{m6}	-.2700**	-.7678**	-.4523**	.0137	-.2554**
	(.0243)	(.1872)	(.1010)	(.1123)	(.0817)
c_{m7}	-.1821**	-.6004**	.2193**	-.3533**	-.2682**
	(.0474)	(.0647)	(.0441)	(.0359)	(.0716)
c_{m8}	-.4416**	-.6695*	.1537*	-.6331**	-.2955**
	(.0741)	(.2995)	(.0652)	(.0740)	(.0509)
c_{m9}	-.0800	.0085	.0501	-.3930**	.4919*
	(.0982)	(.2665)	(.0622)	(.1184)	(.2239)
Years					
d_{m2}	.0240	.0360	.0343	.0093	.0681
	(.0169)	(.0371)	(.0332)	(.0258)	(.0346)
d_{m3}	.0072	.0621	-.0064	.0124	.0936*
	(.0157)	(.0371)	(.0333)	(.0249)	(.0349)
d_{m4}	.0728**	.1673**	.0886*	.0890**	.1466**
	(.0148)	(.0378)	(.0331)	(.0260)	(.0382)
d_{m5}	.0836**	.1603**	.1033**	.1066**	.1922**
	(.0173)	(.0388)	(.0336)	(.0272)	(.0455)
Coefficient of Determination					
R^2	.9929	.9791	.9910	.9814	.9779

*Significant at .05 level.   **Significant at .01 level.

TABLE 11

ESTIMATES OF EQUATION 6.4

	Manufac- tures	Forests	Mines	Animals	Agricul- ture
Intercept					
a_r	6.7201	5.8658	6.7498	3.9850	5.1110
Price Variables					
b_{rr}	- .9851*	- .5936**	-1.0606**	-.2489	-.1257
	(.4280)	(.1700)	(.2270)	(.3109)	(.3246)
b_{rm}	- .0181	- .0271	- .0042	.0661	-.0784
	(.1321)	(.1061)	(.0718)	(.2359)	(.2150)
Regions					
c_{r2}	.1473**	-1.1223**	.2072**	.0238	-.1555*
	(.0280)	(.0647)	(.0302)	(.1284)	(.0683)
c_{r3}	- .6813**	-1.1391**	-1.7013**	-.5952**	-.8922**
	(.0516)	(.0284)	(.0282)	(.0865)	(.0955)
c_{r4}	.2722**	-1.0023**	- .2272**	.6013**	.5361**
	(.0382)	(.0407)	(.0420)	(.0528)	(.0804)
c_{r5}	- .4829**	- .8657**	- .7662**	.6303**	.3826**
	(.0603)	(.0433)	(.0889)	(.1240)	(.0585)
c_{r6}	- .3769**	-1.4579**	-1.1174**	.9014**	.5785**
	(.0193)	(.0771)	(.0522)	(.1053)	(.0624)
c_{r7}	- .0964*	- .4669**	- .6447**	.3300**	.3347**
	(.0376)	(.0266)	(.0228)	(.0336)	(.0547)
c_{r8}	- .4775**	- .5092**	- .7339**	.3940**	.1838**
	(.0588)	(.1233)	(.0337)	(.0694)	(.0388)
c_{r9}	- .1296	.2642*	- .9086**	-.0459	.2407
	(.0779)	(.1098)	(.0321)	(.1110)	(.1710)
Years					
d_{r2}	- .0131	- .0514**	-.0210	-.0728**	-.0090
	(.0133)	(.0152)	(.0171)	(.0242)	(.0264)
d_{r3}	- .0552**	- .1006**	-.1045**	-.1331**	.0023
	(.0124)	(.0153)	(.0172)	(.0233)	(.0267)
d_{r4}	- .0407**	- .0877**	-.1147**	-.1483**	-.0242
	(.0118)	(.0156)	(.0171)	(.0244)	(.0291)
d_{r5}	- .0699**	- .1206**	-.1338**	-.1723**	-.0175
	(.0137)	(.0160)	(.0173)	(.0255)	(.0347)
Coefficient of Determination R^2	.9962	.9976	.9973	.9910	.9897

*Significant at .05 level.   **Significant at .01 level.

and motor carrier demand for agriculture is almost significant (b_{mm}).
Namely, most of the increased explanation of 6.3 and 6.4 above that of 6.1
and 6.2 is provided by the shift variable sets included in the present specification of the model.

One obvious improvement in the present specification relates to the
signs of the price coefficients, especially the own price elasticities.
They are all negative, the expected inverse demand relationship, though not
all of them are significant. The own price elasticities for motor carrier
demand for animal products and the railroad own price elasticities for animal
and agricultural products are particularly suspect, since the parameter estimates are so small with associated large standard errors. Note the estimates for temporal effects. With one exception, the motor carrier demand
functions indicate rising consumption over the 1956-1960 interval and the
railroad demand functions indicate falling consumption over the same interval, with one exception. These temporal trend effects accord well with
known information about transportation consumption trends;[1] moreover, the
temporal estimates display marked non-linearities. Note the almost constant
time trend for railroad demands of agricultural goods movement.

Of the motor carrier price elasticities which are significant, two
are slightly elastic (forests and mines) while the third is mildly inelastic
(manufactures). The two remaining motor carrier elasticities are non-significant, but agriculture is almost significant and it displays mild inelasticity as well. The last one, animal products, is highly inelastic, but its
large standard error precludes meaningful interpretation. Three of the five
cross elasticities have negative signs, indicative of complementary goods,
but their standard errors are so large that no important meaning can be given
to them; this is true of the cross elasticity for mine and animal products,
as well. The only commodity group for which railroad services appear to be
substitutable pertains to the movement of animal products.

Table 11 indicates that the railroad price elasticities are significant for manufactures, forests, and mine products; the first and last
are approximately of unitary elasticity while forest products are rather
inelastic. The small values and high standard errors of the last two own
price elasticities preclude commentary. Also, all the cross elasticities
are almost equal to zero with very large standard errors. Positive signs
are as likely as negative signs here. Obviously, whether motor carriers

---

[1]Total transportation consumption is tabled and graphically portrayed in: U.S., Interstate Commerce Commission, Bureau of Transport
Economics and Statistics, Intercity Ton-Miles 1939-1959, op. cit., Table
1 and Chart 1.

represent complementary or substitutable services is left unanswered.
Lastly, all the temporal shift estimates for the railroad functions display decreasing consumption trends, except the shift variables for agriculture which cluster about zero.

If there are significant decreases in railroad consumption over
time, as is indicated, then why should we obtain negative cross elasticity
signs? Negative cross effects imply complimentarity and, hence, a lack of
competition. Moreover, why should consumption decrease over time, in the
absence of effective substitution, when the output of the economy is rising?
We have no meaningful answers yet. But, it should be clear that the railroad
estimates derived seem to make little theoretical sense. On the other hand,
the significant growth of motor carrier transportation for agricultural
products (19%) is somewhat consistent with mild inelasticity of pricing behavior. On the surface it would appear that railroads retain a rather fixed
share of the agricultural products and this share reflects inelastic pricing
behavior; motor carriers have absorbed the growing transport demands for
agricultural goods, but this excess or new demand represents inelastic
pricing behavior too. This type of explanation results from the interpretation of the estimates obtained, but it does not agree with existing theory.

Similar types of interpretations could be advanced for the estimates
displayed in Tables 10 and 11. It should be clear, however, that much of
transport demand behavior for commodity groups is left unexplained. Our
estimates indicate contradictory results. Therefore, variables of equations 6.3 and 6.4 which appear to be redundant have been deleted. Most of
the explanatory power of 6.3 and 6.4 was provided by the regional variable
set. Therefore, the commodity demand equations were reformulated with prices
and regions such that

$$\text{Log } Q_m = a_m + b_{mm} \text{ Log } P_m + b_{mr} \text{ Log } P_r + \sum_{i=2}^{9} c_{mi} R_i \qquad (6.5)$$

and

$$\text{Log } Q_r = a_r + b_{rm} \text{ Log } P_m + b_{rr} \text{ Log } P_r + \sum_{i=2}^{9} c_{ri} R_i \qquad (6.6)$$

where the R_i are regional dummy variables. Estimates of 6.5 and 6.6 are
provided in Tables 12 and 13.[1]

---

[1]An alternative demand function was fitted, which included prices
and time variables, such as:

$$\text{Log } Q_m = a_m + b_{mm} \text{ Log } P_m + b_{mr} \text{ Log } P_r + \sum_{j=2}^{5} d_j T_j$$

and

Estimates of equations 6.5 and 6.6, represented in Tables 12 and 13, indicate that little explanatory power has been sacrificed in omitting the temporal shift variables. Unfortunately, though, few of the elasticity estimates are significant; it is the regional variable set which is providing most of the model's explanation. Our objective is to derive meaningful elasticity estimates first and then shift variables should account for residual variability. Our results here indicate that the model is behaving conversely.

Compare Tables 10 and 12 for motor carrier demands. Both products of forests and mines display estimates just a bit larger than unitary elasticity. Estimates for manufactures and agriculture have decreased and animals has increased somewhat. The elasticity estimate for agriculture (Table 12) has not changed much from the previous specification and it is almost significant. The greatest alterations in the price elasticities occur in the cross effects, and now two of the cross elasticities are significant. All of the cross elasticities now display negative signs, which is indicative of complementarity. Even those cross effects which have large standard errors would have very low positive values under the most favorable circumstances. It seems quite unlikely that railroads and motor carriers provide little, if any, effective competition for the commodity categories analyzed.

Only one of the railroad elasticity estimates is significant. In fact, none of the other railroad own price or cross price elasticities is near being significant. In comparison with Table 11, all the own price elasticities of Table 13 have decreased in absolute value. Two estimates, animals and agriculture, have shifted signs and there are large errors

$$\text{Log } Q_r = a_r + b_{rm} \text{ Log } P_m + b_{rr} \text{ Log } P_r + \sum_{j=2}^{5} d_j T_j.$$

The R^2 obtained were as follows:

	Manufacturers	Forests	Mines	Animals	Agriculture
Motor Carriers	.1033	.5790	.7159	.0860	.3413
Railroads	.2715	.3187	.0523	.3036	.3210

These R^2 are almost identical to those of Tables 1 and 2. In fact, the parameter estimates of these functions are without exception virtually identical to Tables 8 and 9. Thus the addition of the temporal effects adds little explanation to the basic model and provides identical parameter estimates. In short, the addition of temporal dummies generates redundancies and more reliable temporal parameter estimates are obtained in Tables 10 and 11.

TABLE 12

ESTIMATES OF EQUATION 6.5

	Manufac-tures	Forests	Mines	Animals	Agricul-ture
Intercept					
a_m	9.2049	6.8014	6.8001	6.5304	7.7783
Price Variables					
b_{mm}	-.4263 (.2149)	-1.1664** (.3283)	-1.2530** (.1614)	-.3236 (.2948)	-.5733 (.3046)
b_{mr}	-1.6870** (.4519)	-.5712 (.4681)	-.3133 (.4770)	-.2384 (.3200)	-1.5208** (.3360)
Regions					
c_{m2}	.2441** (.0451)	-.2143 (.1814)	-.0169 (.0669)	-.1927 (.1548)	-.6812** (.0890)
c_{m3}	-.3796** (.0665)	-.6972** (.0865)	-.9448** (.0631)	-.8049** (.1077)	-.4873** (.1101)
c_{m4}	.5627** (.0456)	-.0513 (.1176)	-.0104 (.0920)	.2090** (.0652)	-.6880** (.0930)
c_{m5}	-.2355** (.0782)	-.4877** (.1242)	-.9096** (.1931)	-.0486 (.1503)	-.7065** (.0898)
c_{m6}	-.2527** (.0328)	-.6250** (.2161)	-.4884** (.1149)	.1649 (.1217)	-.4427** (.0768)
c_{m7}	-.0492 (.0486)	-.5430** (.0854)	.2170** (.0520)	-.3952** (.0426)	-.4217** (.0702)
c_{m8}	-.2389** (.0656)	-.4228 (.3082)	.2031** (.0729)	-.4583** (.0748)	-.3206** (.0599)
c_{m9}	.2147* (.0925)	.3686 (.3082)	.0493 (.0727)	-.2967* (.1332)	.9232** (.2022)
Coefficient of Determination					
R^2	.9848	.9576	.9858	.9678	.9629

*Significant at .05 level.   **Significant at .01 level.

TABLE 13

ESTIMATES OF EQUATION 6.6

	Manufac-tures	Forests	Mines	Animals	Agricul-ture
Intercept					
a_r	6.0957	5.7799	6.5589	2.4836	5.0089
Price Variables					
b_{rr}	-.2677 (.3841)	-.3905 (.2550)	-.9097* (.4034)	.3882 (.3946)	.0256 (.2013)
b_{rm}	-.0978 (.1826)	-.0940 (.1788)	.1063 (.1365)	.5017 (.3636)	-.1176 (.1825)
Regions					
c_{r2}	.1221** (.0383)	-1.1947** (.0988)	.1682** (.0565)	.3805 (.1909)	-.1307* (.0533)
c_{r3}	-.7617** (.0565)	-1.1700** (.0471)	-1.7345** (.0534)	-.3977** (.1328)	-.9311** (.0659)
c_{r4}	.2133** (.0387)	-1.0375** (.0641)	-.2207** (.0778)	.6120** (.0804)	.5700** (.0557)
c_{r5}	-.5769** (.0665)	-.9113** (.0676)	-.7628** (.1633)	.6839** (.1853)	.3890** (.0538)
c_{r6}	-.3799** (.0278)	-1.5279** (.1177)	-1.1245** (.0972)	.8497** (.1501)	.6028** (.0460)
c_{r7}	-.1537** (.0413)	-.4907** (.0465)	-.6409** (.0440)	.3676** (.0526)	.3546** (.0420)
c_{r8}	-.5728** (.0558)	-.6291** (.1865)	-.7655** (.0616)	.2395* (.0923)	.1885** (.0359)
c_{r9}	-.2583** (.0786)	.1053 (.1679)	-.8896** (.0615)	-.0247 (.1643)	.1765 (.1211)
Coefficient of Determination					
R^2	.9907	.9915	.9886	.9733	.9894

*Significant at .05 level.   **Significant at .01 level.

associated with the parameters of Table 3. Once again, almost all the
parameter estimates indicate marked inelasticity. Also, cross elasticities for railroad demand display marked complimentarity. The combination
of significant inelasticity and marked complimentarity is consistent with
a declining consumption trend for a maximizing monopolist only.[1] We have
no simple answers. It should be mentioned that the one consistent pattern
emerging from Tables 8 through 13 is the continued unitary elasticity
(approximately) estimates for mine products, both for motor carriers and
railroads. Unfortunately, the cross elasticities for railroads and motor
carriers cluster about zero.

The results obtained from demand estimation for transport services
in terms of commodity groups have been disappointing. Estimates obtained
indicate internal inconsistency and appear lacking in theoretical meaning.
This has resulted in spite of significant explanation in the models utilized.
Application of the basic model for commodity group estimation has paralleled
its use in chapter v. Results obtained from the basic model applied to commodities rival those obtained in the previous chapter.

The Modified Model

Some evidence was presented in chapter v to indicate that there is
transport demand variability by commodity groups. Our efforts to analyze
transport demand by commodity categories have met with little success in
terms of the basic model. Therefore, the elasticity of substitution framework of the modified model will again be introduced for estimation purposes.

First, transport demand will be estimated with only pricing effects
considered. For each commodity group we specify a demand function over all
regions and years such as:

$$\text{Log } (Q_m/Q_r) = a + b \text{ Log } (P_m/P_r) \qquad (6.7)$$

where the elasticity of substitution, b, is estimated separately for each
of five commodity classes. The results of fitting equation 6.7 are presented in Table 14.

Table 14 indicates the wide diversity in explanation provided by
pricing effects alone. The R^2 range from less than 1% to 66%. Only two
of the functions appear to perform tolerably well, mines and agriculture;

---

[1] But the railroads are no longer in the monopoly situation and
that is why our estimates are perplexing. For a brief review of the
changing position of the railroads in the transportation industries see:
Meyer et al., op. cit., chapter i.

TABLE 14

ESTIMATES OF EQUATION 6.7

	Manufac-tures	Forests	Mines	Animals	Agricul-ture
Intercept					
a	1.5745	.1634	.5150	1.7239	.7031
Price Variable					
b	-.6654** (.1277)	-.0592 (.2063)	-1.9248** (.2101)	-.1300 (.2444)	-1.2021** (.1561)
Coefficient of Determination					
R^2	.3869	.0019	.6611	.0065	.5795

**Significant at .01 level.

manufactures represent a distant third. These three functions do provide significant elasticity estimates, though. Manufactures seem quite inelastic and, therefore, indicative of insensitive pricing effects. Conversely, products of mines are highly elastic and extremely sensitive to pricing actions. Agricultural products display near unitary elasticity, which implies a rather stable distribution of market shares subsequent to pricing alterations.

It is clear that transport charges on low valued goods, such as bulk commodities, may represent a substantial share of market price. Therefore, bulk goods are highly responsive to price variations; they are elastic. On the other hand, high valued goods can sustain relatively large transport charges since these costs represent a small fraction of the market price. Thus, high valued goods are price inelastic. These principles apply both to motor carriers and railroads. It is supposed that the railroads have been most effective in retaining bulk traffics, their area of comparative advantage, while motor carriers have been most successful in capturing high value commodities. If this be true, then railroad growth rates should exhibit relative stability for bulk goods and motor carrier trends should exhibit their greatest growth rates amongst the high value commodities.

When we estimate an elasticity of substitution, the elasticity estimate requires a somewhat different interpretation than do elasticity estimates of models which express each price variable explicitly. The elastic

estimate for mine products in Table 14 indicates that major consumption composition shifts result from small price shifts. This implies intermodal competition and technical as well as economic substitutability; this runs counter
to the comparative advantage argument for mine products and railroads. Conversely, the high valued packaged freight area is thought to be most competitive since these commodities yield the highest returns to the transport modes,
due to value of service pricing. Under competitive conditions one would expect a highly elastic estimate in Table 14 for manufactures. Our results are
just the converse. Moreover, compare the temporal effects from Tables 10 and
11 for high and low valued goods. Motor carriers display growth trends for
all commodities, though the rates are differential. The railroads display
greater decreases in forest and mine products than for manufactures and
agricultural goods. In short, the areas of railroad comparative advantage
seem to be losing ground most rapidly and the high valued commodity markets
appear to be where railroads are effectively competing.

Since much variability remains in the model of 6.7 for the three
reasonably poor functions and almost total variation remains in the other
two, the elasticity of substitution model was augmented with two sets of
shift variables. Dummy variable sets for region and time were added such
that

$$\text{Log } (Q_m/Q_r) = a + b \text{ Log } (P_m/P_r) + \sum_{i=2}^{9} c_i R_i + \sum_{j=2}^{5} d_j T_j \qquad (6.8)$$

where the R_i are regions and the T_j are years. Results of fitting 6.8 are
presented in Table 15.

As has been the case previously, the augmented modified model
provides a high degree of explanation. Without exception, all the elasticity estimates have the right signs and three of them are quite significant. Manufactures appear rather inelastic (similar to Table 14) while
forest and mine products are of unitary elasticity, approximately. The
inelastic estimates of Table 14 have been increased while the more
elastic estimates of 6.7 have been decreased in 6.8. Elasticity shifts
for forests, mines, and agriculture are the most striking. Whereas forest products had almost zero elasticity in 6.7, they now have unitary elasticity to near unitary elasticity; agricultural products were mildly elastic
and now appear quite inelastic.

All of the temporal estimates have positive signs and most of the
estimates are significant. This indicates that the consumption ratio,
$\text{Log } (Q_m/Q_r)$, has been increasing over the 1956-1960 interval or motor carriers are capturing an increasing share of the total market for surface
transportation. Compare the time trend estimates in Tables 10 and 11 with

TABLE 15

ESTIMATES OF EQUATION 6.8

	Manufac-tures	Forests	Mines	Animals	Agricul-ture
Intercept					
a	1.4438	.2818	-.2100	2.0645	.7864
Price Variable					
b	-.7014**	-1.0302**	-1.1787**	-.4131	-.4999
	(.2205)	(.1764)	(.1386)	(.3171)	(.3160)
Regions					
c_2	.0258	.5448**	-.2710**	-.1494	-.1447*
	(.0465)	(.0789)	(.0516)	(.1151)	(.0550)
c_3	.1211	.3218	.7191	-.1907	-.0104
	(.0632)	(.0608)	(.0507)	(.1019)	(.1264)
c_4	.1745**	.7512**	.2672**	-.4251**	-.7992**
	(.0321)	(.0546)	(.0573)	(.0801)	(.0876)
c_5	.0338	.1509*	-.0343	-.7620**	-.8935**
	(.0757)	(.0630)	(.1091)	(.1883)	(.0669)
c_6	.1057**	.4194**	.6783**	-.8366**	-.7204
	(.0318)	(.0653)	(.0753)	(.1535)	(.0737)
c_7	-.0780	-.1169	.8640**	-.7062**	-.5095**
	(.0444)	(.0642)	(.0440)	(.0472)	(.0669)
c_8	.0514	-.5990**	.8782**	-.9346**	-.4833**
	(.0396)	(.0937)	(.0437)	(.0674)	(.0589)
c_9	.0675	-.5580**	.9549**	-.3336	.1023
	(.0794)	(.1813)	(.0589)	(.1682)	(.2474)
Years					
d_2	.0391	.0769*	.0543	.0857*	.0874*
	(.0195)	(.0366)	(.0326)	(.0366)	(.0397)
d_3	.0639**	.1518**	.0968**	.1445**	.1081**
	(.0191)	(.0366)	(.0326)	(.0354)	(.0395)
d_4	.1134**	.2421**	.2028**	.2222**	.2089**
	(.0198)	(.0371)	(.0328)	(.0346)	(.0395)
d_5	.1516**	.2956**	.2386**	.2584**	.2673**
	(.0203)	(.0378)	(.0327)	(.0344)	(.0432)
Coefficient of Determination					
R^2	.9208	.9700	.9928	.9669	.9796

*Significant at .05 level.   **Significant at .01 level.

the present estimates in Table 15. The trends displayed in the former tables indicate rather sharp increases in forests, mines, animals, and agriculture for motor carriers, and mild increases in manufactures. On the other hand, railroads display marked reductions in consumption for forests, mines, and animal products and mild reductions in manufactured goods. Agriculture seems to have remained constant. The trend relation of the division of the market between the two modes is portrayed nicely in Table 15. The sharp decreases in rail and marked increases in motor carrier consumption are evidenced in forest, mine, and animal products. Moderate increase in manufactures for motor carriers coupled with moderate decrease for the railroads is jointly reflected in a 15% increase in the ratio of market shares. Agriculture displays a marked increase in the consumption ratio, but the previously cited tables indicate this is the result of sharp motor carrier increases rather than marked railroad decreases.

The persistence of rising consumption ratios, indicative of the increasing role enjoyed by the motor carrier sector, may be the result of scale shifts, pricing behavior, or a combination of the two. Our relatively inelastic price estimates, Table 15, indicate that shifting consumption ratios do not seem to be the result of pricing behavior. This, of course, is surprising. We would expect that the increasing substitutability between railroads and motor carriers would be reflected in increasing price sensitivity over time. This does not seem to be the case.

Most of the explanation provided in estimating the transport demand functions according to equation 6.8 is contributed by the regional dummy variable set. As before, we will omit the temporal dummy set and estimate demand with pricing and regional variables for each commodity group as[1]

$$\text{Log } (Q_m/Q_r) = a + b \text{ Log } (P_m/P_r) + \sum_{i=2}^{9} c_i R_i \qquad (6.9)$$

[1]A demand function with prices and time variables was fitted such as:

$$\text{Log } (Q_m/Q_r) = a + b \text{ Log } (P_m/P_r) + \sum_{j=2}^{5} d_j T_j .$$

The R^2 obtained are as follows:

	Manufactures	Forests	Mines	Animals	Agriculture
R^2 =	.5856	.0597	.6752	.0831	.6353

The elasticity estimates were almost identical with those in Table 14, except the parameter estimate for manufactures, which differs the most, was -.7085. None of the time coefficients were significant. Therefore, the elasticity estimates of the time function replicate the estimates obtained from 6.7 and more meaningful trend estimates are obtained from 6.8.

Five functions such as 6.9 were estimated, one for each commodity group. The results are presented in Table 16.

Only two of the elasticity parameters are significant, forest and mine products. None of the other three elasticity estimates are near significance. Estimates for manufactures, forests, and animal products have been substantially reduced, mine products have remained mildly elastic, and agriculture has switched from a negative sign (expected) to a positive sign. Clearly, little explanatory power has been lost in deleting the temporal dummy variable set, but the significance and near significance of parameter estimates has been reduced.

The positive sign associated with agriculture is not expected nor is it desirable. Only through an increase in the price of motor carrier service, a decrease in the price of railroad service, or a combination of the two can the price ratio increase. Assume that the two transport modes are substitutable. Given a rise in the price ratio, which implies a relative increase in the cost of motor carrier service, we should expect a shift out of motor carrier consumption and into railroad services. This would result in a decline in the consumption ratio or our elasticity estimate would be negative. The elasticity estimate for agriculture is positive (Table 16). This implies that as the relative cost of motor carrier service increases, the relative consumption of motor carrier services for agricultural goods increases by about one-half as much (.4117). Insofar as there is a greater demand for transport service, largely supplied by motor carriers (Table 15),[1] and this increased demand does not adversely affect railroad consumption trends (Table 14), then this excess or increased demand is completely captured by the motor carrier sector. It is difficult to imagine that this increased demand is completely captured in such a singular fashion. The technical substitutability between motor carriers and railroads in the carriage of agricultural goods should be obvious, but our estimates do not indicate economic substituability.

The analysis of transportation demand by commodity classes has resulted in a highly variable set of estimates. Many of the parameter estimates derived from equations 6.1 through 6.9 were significant. In spite of significant explanatory power in the models estimated, there are many estimates which lack theoretical rationale. For example, simple pricing effects (6.7) seem to provide reasonable explanation of consumptive behavior in terms of three commodity classes only, manufactures, mines, and agriculture.

---

[1] Interstate Commerce Commission, Intercity Ton-Miles 1939-1959, op. cit.

TABLE 16

ESTIMATES OF EQUATION 6.9

	Manufactures	Forests	Mines	Animals	Agriculture
Intercept					
a	1.4345	.1407	-.0835	2.1427	.6439
Price Variable					
b	-.1105	-.6090*	-1.3698**	-.1846	.4117
	(.3398)	(.2957)	(.2356)	(.4909)	(.3547)
Regions					
c_2	.1297	.6922**	-.2331*	-.0734	-.1961*
	(.0740)	(.1354)	(.0888)	(.1816)	(.0790)
c_3	.2760**	.4077**	.7545**	-.1251	.3218*
	(.0991)	(.1058)	(.0873)	(.1616)	(.1502)
c_4	.2200**	.8078**	.3183**	-.3779**	-1.0027**
	(.0527)	(.0959)	(.0984)	(.1287)	(.1100)
c_5	.2246	.2449*	.1035	-.6305*	-.7722**
	(.1181)	(.1093)	(.1859)	(.2936)	(.0898)
c_6	.1561**	.5220**	.7629**	-.7311	-.8712**
	(.0523)	(.1131)	(.1288)	(.2402)	(.0963)
c_7	.0191	-.0185	.8573**	-.7136**	-.6311**
	(.0708)	(.1113)	(.0760)	(.0809)	(.0899)
c_8	.1323*	-.4085**	.8802**	-.8991**	-.5631**
	(.0637)	(.1596)	(.0756)	(.1100)	(.0825)
c_9	.2689*	-.1412	.9004**	-.2171	.8001**
	(.1238)	(.3054)	(.1011)	(.2627)	(.2821)
Coefficient of Determination					
R^2	.7431	.8936	.9759	.8895	.9503

*Significant at .05 level.   **Significant at .01 level.

In spite of such explanation the parameter estimates in Table 14 seem too inelastic for manufactures, too elastic for mine products, and quite likely for agricultural products. Theoretically, one would expect estimates similar in magnitude to those obtained, but the manufactures and mine estimates would be reversed.

Addition of dummy variable sets served to indicate regional and temporal variations in transport demand. The latter category results in estimates which agree with commonly held opinions, but they lack statistical significance. Regional variations provide explanatory power but alter parameter estimates drastically, in some cases. In short, the regional influences seem to lack internal consistency. This, of course, could be due to truly differing demand determinants which we have not included. Lastly, there is little if any verification provided from one model specification to the other.

Transportation demand by commodity classes, as here developed, can be described as yielding a set of mixed results. No single model appears to operate well for all commodity groups. For manufactures, simple pricing behavior and time shifts seem to provide the best estimates, about -.70, and regional variability seems to be of minimal importance (see Table 15). The fully augmented modified model yields likely elasticity estimates for forest products, approximately -1.0. Products of mines yield elastic estimates throughout the analysis; in the sense of consistency these are appealing. Estimates for animal products are consistently non-significant, though those obtained are consistently inelastic. Agricultural products provide the greatest variability in obtained estimates. Pricing effects provide mildly elastic estimates, the fully augmented model provides highly inelastic estimates, and the regional model estimates are non-acceptable. Thus, it appears that pricing effects and temporal shifts are the most meaningful ingredients in explaining the agricultural sector.

Apparently, different causative agents are operative in the system. Whereas significant amounts of national transportation consumption could be explained in terms of the basic or modified models with some internal verification, results of the present chapter are much more disparate. Pricing behavior does not seem to provide the major or sufficient answer to inter-carrier competition in terms of the five commodity groups analyzed.

Two questions in particular are suggested by our results. First, the disparate nature of results obtained in this chapter suggest that the non-price characteristics of transportation may be more important. Though qualitative differences do exist for transport services these are usually reflected in transport costs. Thus, we do not feel that the qualitative characteristics of transportation would cause the disparate set of results obtained. More likely, though, is the commodity classification used. Our economy is primarily an aggregation of specialized regional economic structures. Each region would generate its own set of transport demands based on regional specializations in production. Therefore, if demand by commodity group has meaning it should be reflected in regional transport demands and regional-commodity combinations. These issues we shall now investigate.

CHAPTER VII

MESO ANALYSIS BY REGIONS

In our previous analyses, primarily chapter v, evidence was presented to indicate that transportation demand displays some marked regional
variations.[1] The present chapter is an attempt to clarify the nature of
this spatial variability. Of course, production sites and consumption sites
do not necessarily coincide. In fact, much of the output of the economy
(supply) is provided at locations quite distant from major centers of consumption (demand) because there is regional specialization in production.[2]
The spatial units which we must utilize in this study are fixed. Their delimitation is beyond our control and they may not be too meaningful from
the viewpoint of either demand or supply.[3] If transportation demand varies
regionally, as we suspect, and if the set of nine regions being utilized is
a meaningful set, then the estimation of transportation demand variability
by areal units should be feasible. This is what we now attempt.

The Basic Model

A research strategy was outlined previously and applied as two alternative models.[4] That design will be followed again in the present analysis
so that comparability of results will be insured. Since our basic input information is based on nine regional divisions (groups of states), we shall
attempt to estimate transport demand for each region. The basic set of input data contains information of five commodity groups over a five-year interval. Thus, there will be twenty-five observations available in each re-
tional demand function.

---

[1] See Tables 2 and 5 in chapter v and the associated discussion there.

[2] For an exposition of location theory, see: Isard, Location and
Space-Economy, op. cit., and Hoover, op. cit., especially chapters ii, iii
and iv.

[3] The exact converse exists when one is dealing with areal data and
variable boundaries. Here the object is to generate a meaningful set of
regions. Optimization methods exist for the solution of such a problem. For
one such example, see: B. J. L. Berry, "A Method for Deriving Multi-Factor
Uniform Regions," Przeglad Geograficzny (Polish Geographical Review) XXXIII,
No. 2 (1961), 263-279.

[4] See chapter iv, The Basic Model and the Modified Basic Model.

Following the basic model of equation 4.9, separate demand functions for motor carriers and railroads are specified for each region such that

$$\text{Log } Q_m = a_m + b_{mm} \text{ Log } P_m + b_{mr} \text{ Log } P_r \qquad (7.1)$$

and

$$\text{Log } Q_r = a_r + b_{rm} \text{ Log } P_m + b_{rr} \text{ Log } P_r \qquad (7.2)$$

where m and r refer to motor carriers and railroads, respectively. Once again, notice that the basic model attempts to account for consumption in terms of pricing effects alone. Results of equations 7.1 and 7.2 are presented in Tables 17 and 18 where the standard errors of the estimated coefficients are in parenthesis.[1]

Estimates derived from 7.1 and 7.2 display several interesting characteristics. First, the amount of consumption variation accounted for in the model is quite variable. Some functions look quite good, such as motor carrier demand or railroad demand in the Northwestern Region. On the other hand, much variability remains for motor carrier and railroad demands in the Pacific Region. Briefly, the range of R_2 is very broad, indeed. Secondly, a large number of the estimated parameters are significant, especially for the motor carrier demand functions. Thirdly, there is a notable lack of symmetry in the cross effects.

All of the motor carrier elasticities in Table 17 have the correct sign (-)[2] and all the pertinent cross effects have positive signs, indicative of railroad substitutability. On the other hand, only six of the nine railroad demand functions (Table 18) have the correct sign and all the cross effects have negative signs, indicative of complementarity. This type of asymmetry in the cross effects was noted in the macro analysis of chapter v and was thought suspicious there. It is suspect here as well. Notice the motor carrier estimates of Table 17. Except for the Pacific Region, which is a totally unreliable estimate, all of the own price elasticities are quite elastic. In fact, some of the estimates seem unduly large. Coupled with the large own price elasticities are quite large cross elasticities. On the surface, one would suspect that these two services, motor carriers and railroads, are highly competitive, where

---

[1]Standard errors are enclosed in parenthesis and placed directly under the estimated coefficients. This format will be followed throughout the chapter.

[2]Reference to chapter ii will serve to establish the inverse quantity-price relationship of demand theory.

TABLE 17

ESTIMATES OF EQUATION 7.1

Coefficient		Southern	Middle Atlantic	New England	Central	North Western	Mid-Western	South Western	Rocky Mountain	Pacific
Intercept	a_m	6.3613	7.2627	6.1550	7.6027	8.6498	8.0817	6.2860	7.0226	6.8683
Prices	b_{mm}	-1.9094**	-4.0330**	-2.8339**	-3.9544**	-4.5977**	-4.0775**	-3.2106**	-3.6035**	-.1102
		(.4569)	(.9161)	(.8381)	(.5987)	(.6107)	(.7753)	(.3189)	(.8313)	(1.159)
	b_{mr}	2.1310**	3.0906**	2.1000**	3.4089**	1.6833**	2.3427**	3.5847**	2.6801*	-.5373
		(.5025)	(.7494)	(.4945)	(.4657)	(.1750)	(.4468)	(.3945)	(.9671)	(1.1468)
Coefficient	R^2	.4796	.5462	.4704	.7185	.8388	.5997	.8274	.5191	.1027

*Significant at .05 level.

**Significant at .01 level.

TABLE 18

ESTIMATES OF EQUATION 7.2

Coefficient		Southern	Middle Atlantic	New England	Central	North Western	Mid-Western	South Western	Rocky Mountain	Pacific
Intercept	a_r	7.6391	10.008	6.0685	7.7767	8.3625	6.6258	6.2891	6.3645	5.8109
Prices	b_{rr}	-.9604* (.4479)	-1.9300* (.8318)	-.2639 (.4708)	.4138 (.5020)	-.7260** (.1104)	-.0344 (.4253)	.2278 (.4728)	-1.2953** (.3701)	.4046 (1.1344)
	b_{rm}	-1.5565** (.4072)	-3.6199** (1.0167)	-1.7232* (.7980)	-2.6363** (.6454)	-2.8072** (.3853)	-1.5491* (.7380)	-1.3623** (.3821)	.1922 (.3182)	-1.6549 (1.1471)
Coefficient	R^2	.7648	.5620	.2934	.5678	.8654	.2782	.5387	.7696	.3126

*Significant at .05 level.

**Significant at .01 level.

small price changes induce large consumption alterations. The magnitudes of
the cross elasticities further support the view that the railroads are extremely good competitors.

The major superficial inference from Table 18 is that motor carriers
and railroads offer virtually identical services. That is, they are complementary goods which satisfy similar demands and are consumed jointly. Only
four of the nine demand functions have significant own price elasticities, while
seven of the nine cross elasticities are significant. Moreover, in eight of
the nine cases the absolute magnitudes of the cross effects are greater than
the own price elasticities, while seven of the nine cross elasticities are
significant. Moreover, in eight of the nine cases the absolute magnitudes
of the cross effects are greater than the own price elasticities, which are
rather inelastic. It seems rather strange that a complementary cross effect
should be more sensitive to small price changes than an own price elasticity.

We are not fully content with the estimates from 7.1 and 7.2 for several
reasons. Price elasticities displayed in Table 17 seem too large, in absolute
value, both for own and cross price effects. The cross price elasticities
of Table 18 seem too large given the estimates obtained for the own price
elasticities. Lastly, the marked asymmetry for cross effects between demand
functions for each mode enhances our suspicions. Obviously, the explanation
afforded by pricing effects alone leaves much residual variability in consumption.

Given our doubts about the estimates from equations 7.1 and 7.2, the
basic model was augmented with variable sets for commodity groups and observation years. That is, dummy variables were added to the basic model to represent commodities and the time span of observations within each region. Thus,

$$\text{Log } Q_m = a_m + b_{mm} \text{ Log } P_m + b_{mr} \text{ Log } P_r + \sum_{J=2}^{5} d_{mj} T_j + \sum_{k=2}^{5} f_{mk} Z_k \tag{7.3}$$

and

$$\text{Log } Q_r = a_r + b_{rm} \text{ Log } P_m + b_{rr} \text{ Log } P_r + \sum_{j=2}^{5} d_{rj} T_j + \sum_{k=2}^{5} f_{rk} Z_k \tag{7.4}$$

where each equation describes transport demand, by mode, as a function of
prices, time, and commodities handled. Estimates of 7.3 and 7.4 are presented in Tables 19 and 20, respectively.

Without exception, all of the R^2 of Tables 19 and 20 are larger
than was the case in the previous two tables. All demand functions in the
present case have R_2 equal to or greater than .99 and this seems too good
to be true. Notice that most of the commodity variables are significant
in both tables and some of the time variables are significant. All of the

TABLE 19

ESTIMATES OF EQUATION 7.3

Coefficient		Southern	Middle Atlantic	New England	Central	North Western	Mid-Western	South Western	Rocky Mountain	Pacific
Intercept	a_m	8.8776	7.3679	7.3637	8.9488	8.3414	8.2726	8.8538	7.0702	7.8205
Prices	b_{mm}	-1.3168**	-.5402*	-1.0362**	-.8177*	-1.0483*	-1.2289**	-.9603**	-1.6736**	-1.2241**
		(.2177)	(.2439)	(.2021)	(.3002)	(.4433)	(.2963)	(.2886)	(.3601)	(.2399)
	b_{mr}	-.3715	.5443	.2481	-.4770	-.6804	-.1733	-.9432	1.2478	.4249
		(.1982)	(.3050)	(.5438)	(.5479)	(.8695)	(.9579)	(.5982)	(.6088)	(.6593)
Commodities										
z_2	f_{m2}	-2.0455**	-2.4474**	-1.8840**	-2.6804**	-2.2013**	-2.4081**	-2.6848**	-2.1018**	-1.7268**
		(.0972)	(.0740)	(.2466)	(.2215)	(.4234)	(.1589)	(.3066)	(.1144)	(.0428)
z_3	f_{m3}	-2.0754**	-1.5763**	-1.9442**	-2.3750**	-2.7010**	-2.0754**	-1.7719**	-.7527	-1.3198**
		(.1890)	(.1547)	(.3219)	(.4066)	(.8197)	(.6172)	(.4208)	(.3956)	(.3695)
z_4	f_{m4}	-.7838**	-1.6505**	-1.4067**	-1.2516**	-.5854*	-.6049	-1.0681**	-1.1087**	-1.4614**
		(.1094)	(.0252)	(.0802)	(.1441)	(.2340)	(.4456)	(.1758)	(.2778)	(.1659)
z_5	f_{m5}	-1.3034**	-1.8597**	-1.6183**	-2.2969**	-1.6018**	-1.2223**	-1.5572**	-.8046**	-1.0122**
		(.0371)	(.0814)	(.0891)	(.1880)	(.2388)	(.2032)	(.1340)	(.1253)	(.1114)
Years										
T_2	d_{m2}	.0466*	-.0240	.0357	-.0374	.0486	.0855	.0289	.1024	-.0244
		(.017)	(.023)	(.049)	(.025)	(.049)	(.046)	(.043)	(.052)	(.041)
T_3	d_{m3}	.0239	.0258	.0102	-.0420	.0922*	.0164	.0661	.0665	-.0989*
		(.020)	(.026)	(.041)	(.026)	(.046)	(.045)	(.044)	(.050)	(.038)
T_4	d_{m4}	.1043**	.1026**	.0287	.0434	.1695**	.0936	.1485**	.1482**	.0022
		(.027)	(.023)	(.038)	(.024)	(.041)	(.047)	(.047)	(.051)	(.034)
T_5	d_{m5}	.0880*	.1367**	.0103	.0514	.2472*	.0998	.1418**	.1288*	.0891*
		(.036)	(.026)	(.041)	(.032)	(.053)	(.050)	(.048)	(.057)	(.035)
Coefficient	R^2	.9990	.9990	.9965	.9989	.9965	.9966	.9964	.9951	.9961

*Significant at .05 level.   **Significant at .01 level.

TABLE 20

ESTIMATES OF EQUATION 7.4

Coefficient		Southern	Middle Atlantic	New England	Central	North Western	Mid-Western	South Western	Rocky Mountain	Pacific
Intercept	a_r	6.4720	6.0260	5.1076	5.9280	6.2868	5.5942	6.6663	5.7366	6.7692
Prices	b_{rr}	-.4734 (.2542)	-.1338 (.2619)	-.2216 (.4850)	-.2425 (.5259)	-.4882 (.4780)	-.6983 (.7446)	-1.0435* (.4432)	-.5237 (.2989)	-1.1173** (.3220)
	b_{rm}	-.2046 (.2792)	.0907 (.2094)	.2236 (.1802)	.3106 (.2882)	-.6414* (.2437)	.4491 (.2303)	.0334 (.2138)	-.0101 (.1768)	-.0772 (.1171)
Commodities										
	z_2	-.4614** (.1247)	-1.7497** (.0635)	-.8189** (.2199)	-1.6817** (.2126)	-.6591** (.2327)	-1.7694** (.1235)	-1.1014** (.2271)	-.5186 (.0561)	-.0643** (.0209)
	z_3	.1138 (.2425)	.4415** (.1329)	-.5776 (.2871)	.1798 (.3903)	.1817 (.4506)	-.4559 (.4798)	-.5894 (.3118)	-.0497 (.1942)	-.9435** (.1805)
	z_4	-1.8608** (.1404)	-2.1490** (.0216)	-1.9144** (.0715)	-1.6974** (.1383)	-.6206** (.1286)	-.6315 (.3464)	-1.4332** (.1303)	-.9300** (.1364)	-1.5614** (.0810)
	z_5	-.8242** (.0476)	-1.1481** (.0699)	-1.0024** (.0795)	-.6036** (.1804)	.1245 (.1313)	-.1096 (.1580)	-.5643** (.0993)	-.1416* (.0615)	-.1876** (.0544)
Years										
	T_2	-.0357 (.022)	-.0646** (.020)	-.0836 (.044)	-.0618 (.024)	-.0472 (.027)	-.0299 (.035)	-.0656 (.032)	-.0168 (.025)	.0026 (.020)
	T_3	-.0965** (.026)	-.1623** (.023)	-.1465** (.036)	-.1277** (.024)	-.1073** (.025)	-.0068 (.035)	-.0748* (.033)	-.0357 (.024)	-.0189 (.018)
	T_4	-.0976* (.035)	-.1544** (.020)	-.1619** (.034)	-.1195** (.023)	-.0966** (.022)	-.0195 (.037)	-.0905* (.034)	-.0481 (.025)	-.0159 (.016)
	T_5	-.1066* (.047)	-.1709** (.022)	-.1807** (.036)	-.1109** (.030)	-.0823* (.029)	-.0308 (.039)	-.1199* (.036)	-.0663* (.028)	-.0475* (.017)
Coefficient	R^2	.9990	.9994	.9959	.9987	.9978	.9959	.9964	.9962	.9992

*Significant at .05 level. **Significant at .01 level.

own price elasticities have the correct sign (-), but the cross effects display both positive and negative signs.

In Table 17 all the price elasticities (except the Pacific Region) had rather large values, which we suspected as being biased. In Table 19 only the own price elasticities are significant and all the large parameter estimates have been drastically reduced. Now most of the elasticities closely approximate unitary elasticity. None of the cross price effects are significant, though the Rocky Mountain cross effect approximates significance, and their absolute magnitudes are quite small relative to Table 17. Most of the explanation beyond pricing effects seems attributable to the commodity variable set, of which most estimates are highly significant. Little can be said about the signs of the cross effects since the standard errors are so large. For example, the Northwestern, Mid-Western, and Southwestern demand functions have standard errors associated with the cross effects of such large magnitudes that the true sign may be positive. Conversely, cross elasticity estimates such as those for New England and the Pacific may be negative.

Whereas almost all the price elasticities were significant in Table 18, they are now almost all non-significant, as seen in Table 20. Of course, most of the consumption variability has been explained in the functions of Table 20, but this is due to the commodity variables, primarily. Some of the time variables appear to provide additional explanation. The rather large price elasticities of Table 18 have been reduced in Table 20, but there is no clear pattern of change for the entire set of own price elasticities. All one can say is that the parameter estimates now display correct signs and large standard errors. The cross effects have such small values (except for the Northwestern Region) and such large standard errors that the signs of the cross effects could be either positive or negative in most cases.

The augmented basic model, equations 7.3 and 7.4, drastically reduces some of the very large estimates of the basic model, equations 7.1 and 7.2. Furthermore, appreciable additional explanation is provided by the augmented model. Most of the additional explanation, above pricing effects, seems to be attributable to the dummy variable set of commodities. Much of the significance of the elasticity estimates has been lost in the conversion from the basic model to the augmented model. Also, the behavior and interpretation of coefficient signs has been left indeterminate.

In an effort to eliminate redundancy, achieve more meaningful elasticity estimates, and still obtain sufficient explanation, a third variant of the basic model was estimated. In the present specification, transport consumption is viewed as a function of prices and commodity variations in each region, such that

$$Log\ Q_m = a_m + b_{mm}\ Log\ P_m + b_{mr}\ Log\ P_r + \sum_{k=2}^{5} f_{mk}Z_k \qquad (7.5)$$

and

$$Log\ Q_r = a_r + b_{rm}\ Log\ P_m + b_{rr}\ Log\ P_r + \sum_{k=2}^{5} f_{rk}Z_k \qquad (7.6)$$

where each equation refers to a transport mode and nine such pairs are estimated for the regions. Results are displayed in Tables 21 and 22.

Very little reduction in explanation results from the estimation
of equations 7.5 and 7.6 as contrasted with the fully augmented model of
equations 7.3 and 7.4. Most of the explanation provided in Tables 19 and
20, beyond pricing effects, was attributable to the commodity variable set,
as noted in Tables 21 and 22. Also, note that the signs of all the commodity
variables in Table 21 are negative. This indicates that the effective level
of motor carrier demand is lower for all commodity groups relative to manufactures. Negative commodity signs are prevalent for railroads too with
the exception of Z_3, mine products. Essentially, mine products in the
Southern, Middle Atlantic, Central, Southwestern, and Rocky Mountain Regions
represent higher levels of railroad consumption than do manufactures. Otherwise, all other commodity groups have lower consumption levels. These exceptional regions are the coal producers and virtually all coal output is
transported by the railroads.

Own price elasticities in Table 21 are of similar magnitude as
those of Table 19, with a few exceptions. Conversely, the cross effects
of Tables 19 and 21 display marked changes. Only two of the cross effects
in Table 21 have positive signs, which represents a radical shift from the
pricing results of Table 17. Four of the significant own price elasticities
are close to unity, but three of the four significant cross effects are appreciably greater than unity in absolute value; also, they have negative
signs associated with them. This superficial evidence for complementarity
is disturbing, especially since it is in such sharp contrast to the evidence
of Table 17.

Railroad estimates in Table 22 are equally as poor as those in
Table 20. Few of the price elasticities are significant, their standard
errors are unduly large, and little can be inferred about the substitutability of modes. Though two of the own price elasticities have positive
signs, their standard errors are several times larger than the elasticity
estimates; therefore, the true signs may be negative. Alternatively, some
of the standard errors associated with own price elasticities of negative
sign are so large as to preclude confidence.

TABLE 21

ESTIMATES OF EQUATION 7.5

Coefficient		Southern	Middle Atlantic	New England	Central	North Western	Mid-Western	South Western	Rocky Mountain	Pacific
Intercept	a_m	9.6665	7.9267	7.1785	10.0911	9.1335	8.8850	10.2781	7.7557	8.3890
Prices	b_{mm}	-1.7099** (.2197)	-.1350 (.4159)	-.9673** (.1510)	-.8415* (.3581)	-.1065 (.4211)	-1.2141** (.3200)	-.9721** (.3274)	-1.8962** (.3278)	-.6542* (.2429)
	b_{mr}	-.7025** (.1878)	-.3786 (.3567)	.3828 (.3384)	-1.5666** (.4176)	-2.1078* (.8018)	-.7809 (.8569)	-2.2655** (.5707)	.9155 (.6586)	-.5637 (.7057)
Commodities										
z_2	f_{m2}	-2.1853** (.1040)	-2.6831** (.1153)	-1.8324** (.1633)	-3.0976** (.1829)	-3.0051** (.3500)	-2.4711** (.1642)	-3.3543** (.2943)	-2.0314** (.1084)	-1.6648** (.0522)
z_3	f_{m3}	-2.4867** (.1201)	-1.9295** (.1930)	-1.8544** (.1931)	-3.1859** (.3012)	-4.0476** (.7565)	-2.4781** (.5399)	-2.5498** (.4178)	-1.0364* (.3892)	-1.5581* (.4521)
z_4	f_{m4}	-.5500** (.0764)	-1.6278** (.0437)	-1.4321** (.0534)	-.9845** (.1168)	-.3218 (.2665)	-.3118 (.3766)	-.8913** (.1910)	-.9031** (.2643)	-1.3295** (.2000)
z_5	f_{m5}	-1.2469** (.0426)	-2.1389** (.1120)	-1.6458** (.0572)	-2.6379** (.1621)	-2.0421** (.2052)	-1.3253** (.2001)	-1.8327** (.1374)	-.8037** (.1393)	-.8068** (.1136)
Coefficient	R^2	.9974	.9960	.9963	.9979	.9891	.9946	.9929	.9918	.9903

*Significant at .05 level.   **Significant at .01 level.

TABLE 22

ESTIMATES OF EQUATION 7.6

Coefficients		Southern	Middle Atlantic	New England	Central	North Western	Mid-Western	South Western	Rocky Mountain	Pacific
Intercept	a_r	5.5907	6.2970	4.5629	5.5963	6.5407	5.4756	5.5127	5.3246	6.7073
Prices	b_{rr}	-.0379 (.2114)	.0644 (.4329)	.1800 (.5553)	-.0685 (.5656)	-.6927 (.4372)	-.5757 (.5527)	-.1374 (.4013)	-.3708 (.2998)	-.9578** (.2834)
	b_{rm}	.1693 (.2473)	-.5285 (.5048)	.2306 (.2477)	.3755 (.4850)	-.7644*** (.2297)	.4355* (.2064)	.2040 (.2303)	.1890 (.1492)	-.2211* (.0975)
Commodities										
z_2	f_{r2}	-.2685* (.1171)	-1.5766** (.1400)	-.6306* (.2679)	-1.6227*** (.2478)	-.7020*** (.1909)	-1.7534*** (.1059)	-.6398*** (.2070)	-.5773** (.0493)	-.0777*** (.0209)
z_3	f_{r3}	.5671** (.1352)	.4157 (.2343)	-.3470 (.3168)	.3385 (.4080)	-.0097 (.4125)	-.3772 (.3483)	.0334 (.2938)	.1274 (.1772)	-.9399** (.1815)
z_4	f_{r4}	-2.1129*** (.0861)	-2.1460*** (.0530)	-1.9510** (.0876)	-1.7559*** (.1582)	-.5286*** (.1453)	-.6880* (.2494)	-1.6301*** (.1343)	-1.0675*** (.1203)	-1.5699*** (.0803)
z_5	f_{r5}	-.8766** (.0480)	-.9997** (.1359)	-1.0506** (.0939)	-.5588* (.2195)	.0954 (.1119)	-.0862 (.1290)	-.4165** (.0966)	-.1646* (.0634)	-.2273** (.0456)
Coefficient	R^2	.9981	.9954	.9855	.9950	.9932	.9955	.9935	.9944	.9987

*Significant at .05 level.   **Significant at .01 level.

One tentative conclusion may be advanced, however, based upon the estimates of equations 7.5 and 7.6. Appreciable transport demand variability seems to exist on the regional basis being utilized and it appears to be substantially influenced by the types of commodities handled. This conclusion is not intuitively surprising. Relative to the estimates obtained in the past two chapters,[1] results of this type are rewarding, because they provide reason to probe further.

Application of the basic model at several levels of analysis has yielded a variety of results. Our present results are in many ways superior to those obtained in chapters v and vi. Pricing effects alone, as is evident in Tables 17 and 18, provide greater explanation in the regional analysis than in either of the two previous chapters. Nevertheless, pricing effects leave much consumption behavior unexplained. The introduction of dummy variable sets for commodity groups and time paths (Tables 19 and 20) increases explanation considerably. Yet estimated coefficients display inconsistent behavior under minor modifications of the basic model, as witnessed by a comparison of Tables 17-22. Since estimation and explanation, not prediction, is our primary focus we are not content with the results.

The Modified Model

Since many of the estimates of the basic model yield indeterminate results for point estimates, signs, and significance tests, we resort to the modified model of equation 4.11 and the elasticity of substitution. Once more, this model specification relates relative quantities consumed with relative prices charged. It is

$$\text{Log } (Q_m/Q_r) = a + b \text{ Log } (P_m/P_r) \tag{7.7}$$

where m and r refer to the two modes, motor carriers and railroads. In each of nine regions one demand function was fitted, such as 7.7, where consumptive relations are viewed solely as a function of relative prices. Results for equation 7.7 are presented in Table 23.

Obviously, the model of 7.7 performs quite well for some regions while other regions fare poorly. Both the Northwestern and Mid-Western Regions result in high R^2, while the Southern and Pacific Regions yield

---

[1]Recall that the meso analysis of chapter vi was not able to isolate adequately the differences in transport demand by commodity groups. But that analysis was on a national basis with dummy variables for regions. Here we are analyzing the regions with commodity variations expressed in terms of dummy variables.

TABLE 23

ESTIMATES OF EQUATION 7.7

Coefficient		Southern	Middle Atlantic	New England	Central	North Western	Mid-Western	South Western	Rocky Mountain	Pacific
Intercept	a	1.1259	1.4357	1.3064	1.6332	.9017	1.2851	1.1918	1.2178	1.5946
Prices	b	-1.2126	-3.4388**	-2.3267**	-2.9370**	-2.4160**	-2.3620**	-1.9505**	-3.3628**	1.1903
		(.7934)	(.7588)	(.3940)	(.5233)	(.2012)	(.2085)	(.4642)	(.6822)	(1.1417)
Coefficient	R^2	.0921	.4716	.6025	.5779	.8624	.8479	.4342	.5136	.0451

**Significant at .01 level.

poor fits. Except for the Southern and Pacific regions, the proportion of explained variation is reasonably high for all regions and all the elasticity estimates are highly significant. The two exceptions, previously mentioned, yield such poor results that little can be said about estimates obtained for them.

Elasticity estimates are of equally large magnitudes as those seen in Tables 17 and 18. Though seven of the nine are statistically significant, all seven appear unusually elastic. These estimates indicate that consumptive choices for transportation are highly sensitive to small price changes and, therefore, motor carriers and railroads are effective substitutes. If the issue were so well defined our results from the basic model should have confirmed our present estimates. However, it was noted earlier in this chapter that under certain simple modifications and sensitivity of consumption to pricing effects was less than well defined. We are highly dubious about accepting the estimates of Table 23 as they stand.

It is pleasing to note that eight of the nine elasticity estimates of equation 7.7 have the right sign. The combination of proper sign, statistical significance, and relatively good explanatory power lends reliability to the further use of the modified model. But we have expressed reservations about the estimates of Table 23. Therefore, the modified model will be augmented through the addition of dummy variable sets for commodity groups and time. Symbolically,

$$\text{Log } (Q_m/Q_r) = a + b \text{ Log } (P_m/P_r) + \sum_{j=2}^{5} d_j T_j + \sum_{k=2}^{5} f_k Z_k \qquad (7.8)$$

where the T_j are years and the Z_k are commodity groups. Results for equation 7.8 are presented in Table 24.

The augmented modified model indicates that less than 1% of the consumption variability is left unexplained in all regions. For the Southern and Pacific Regions this represents an extraordinary increase in explanatory power, and for all other regions it is an appreciable increase. With the exception of the Northwest, all elasticity estimates are significant. Without exception all of the commodity parameters are significant and a majority of the temporal effects are significant. This is an impressive collection of evidence.

One of the major doubts expressed about the results of Table 23 was the seemingly excessive magnitudes of the elasticity coefficients. It is clear in Table 24 that all the elasticity estimates have been appreciably reduced in magnitude, all have the correct sign, and eight of the nine are statistically significant. Whereas almost all such estimates were highly

TABLE 24

ESTIMATES OF EQUATION 7.8

Coefficient		Southern	Middle Atlantic	New England	Central	North Western	Mid-Western	South Western	Rocky Mountain	Pacific
Intercept	a	1.3383	1.3861	1.4656	1.6118	1.4154	1.5957	1.2681	1.4504	1.4831
Prices	b	-.5696**	-.6497*	-1.1144**	-.8675**	-.4859	-1.7164**	-.7787**	-1.6949**	-1.1289**
		(.1853)	(.2345)	(.1677)	(.2746)	(.5039)	(.2411)	(.2067)	(.3121)	(.2550)
Commodities										
z_2	f_2	-1.3857**	-.6978**	-.7896**	-.6063**	-1.2635**	-.5122**	-1.2363**	-1.5723**	-1.6508**
		(.1066)	(.0947)	(.1106)	(.1423)	(.3350)	(.1031)	(.1071)	(.0940)	(.0419)
z_3	f_3	-1.6159**	-2.0346**	-.9754**	-1.6214**	-2.2450**	-.8318**	-.6678**	-.7588**	-.6237**
		(.0317)	(.0709)	(.0701)	(.0741)	(.4787)	(.1098)	(.0358)	(.0575)	(.0368)
z_4	f_4	.7516**	.4996**	.4230**	.1141**	-.1675*	-.5458**	.1770*	-.1400*	.2092**
		(.0366)	(.0295)	(.0431)	(.0244)	(.0737)	(.0677)	(.0780)	(.0672)	(.0359)
z_5	f_5	-.5570**	-.7150**	-.7154**	-1.3855**	-1.5657**	-.9082**	-.9044**	-.6674**	-.7664**
		(.0398)	(.0973)	(.0399)	(.1322)	(.1840)	(.1062)	(.1016)	(.1331)	(.0753)
Years										
T_2	d_2	.0904**	.0411	.0822	.0076	.0855	.1011*	.1145**	.1204*	-.0139
		(.025)	(.029)	(.040)	(.023)	(.055)	(.036)	(.036)	(.056)	(.039)
T_3	d_3	.1542**	.1897**	.1373**	.0654	.1827**	-.0231	.1679**	.1028	-.0702
		(.026)	(.029)	(.038)	(.024)	(.049)	(.037)	(.035)	(.055)	(.037)
T_4	d_4	.2657**	.2575**	.1844**	.1633**	.2587**	.1317**	.2685**	.1951**	.0257
		(.026)	(.030)	(.038)	(.023)	(.046)	(.037)	(.036)	(.055)	(.035)
T_5	d_5	.2928**	.3066**	.2095**	.2089**	.3489**	.1613**	.2961**	.1919**	.1392**
		(.026)	(.032)	(.039)	(.024)	(.056)	(.036)	(.035)	(.057)	(.037)
Coefficient	R^2	.9987	.9985	.9956	.9988	.9969	.9960	.9955	.9911	.9952

*Significant at .05 level.   **Significant at .01 level.

elastic previously (Table 23), only two estimates, the Rocky Mountain and
Mid-Western Regions, are highly elastic now. Two estimates, the New England
and Pacific Regions, are essentially of unitary elasticity and the Central
and Southwestern Regions display mild inelasticity. The Southern and
Middle Atlantic Regions display marked inelasticity and the last region,
Northwestern, had such a large standard error that little can be said
about it.

Many of the temporal estimates are significant and they clearly display a pattern of non-linearity. Almost all the time coefficients have positive signs, which indicates that the share of traffic carried by motor carriers has been increasing over the 1956-1960 interval. Given a level of output
for the economy and its derived transportation demands, then an increase in
the transport share for motor carriers can result from a decreased railroad
consumption, an increased motor carrier consumption, or a combination of
the two. The total output of the economy has been persistently increasing
over the post-war interval with concomitant increases in derived transport
demands.[1] Over this same time interval both the railroads and the motor carriers have displayed increasing consumption of their respective services.[2]
But differential consumptive behavior in the economy has caused the quantity
ratio, Log (Q_m/Q_r), to rise. There does not appear to be a secular decline
in railroad consumption. Rather, the increase in motor carrier consumption
has far exceeded railroad increases. Thus, we note marked increases in the
temporal coefficients of Table 24.

Also, observe that the time coefficients associated with elastic
price estimates display the smallest growth rates. Those consumption ratios
which display the largest increases are associated with the relatively inelastic estimates. For example, the Rocky Mountain and Mid-Western Regions
have price elasticities of -1.69 and -1.71; their total consumption ratio
increase at the end of 1960 was 19% and 16%, respectively. Conversely, the
inelastic price estimates of the Southern and Middle Atlantic Regions have
consumption ratio increases of 29% and 30%, respectively.

The observed association between elasticity estimates and consumption

---

[1]Almost all of the post-war economic series indicate rising output
levels. Depending upon one's inclinations as well as the object of use,
such measures as GNP, the Index of Industrial Production, income per capita,
etc., may be used to indicate this secular growth trend. Many of these
series can be found in: U.S. Department of Commerce, Office of Business
Economics, Survey of Current Business, op. cit.

[2]U.S. Interstate Commerce Commission, Transport Statistics in the
United States, op. cit., Part I; Railroads, Part 7: Motor Carriers, annual.

ratios makes much theoretical sense. That is, given a situation where railroads and motor carriers represent effective substitutes for one another, then
their competitive behavior will be discernible from their pricing policies.
If they are truly effective substitutes then minor price changes will re-
allocate much of the consumption.[1] Neither of the modes will desire to price
itself out of the market through price increases; therefore, two situations
may result. Either they share the available market on individual cost and
pricing considerations or they collude. The latter alternative is extra-
legal and we shall not consider it as a viable outcome.[2]

If the elasticity of substitution estimate indicates that two modes
are effective substitutes in transportation consumption (b is elastic), then
consumption will be very sensitive to minor price alterations. Since neither
mode wishes to relinquish its traffic, a natural consumption sharing outcome
will result, based upon cost and pricing considerations. Though the over-all
demand for transport services may increase over time the allocation of the
total market, the consumption composition, will not alter much.[3] Therefore,
under effective competition one does not expect major changes in mode composition for transport inputs. Growth rates will remain relatively stable under
elastic conditions, too (see Table 24).

Alternatively, inelastic price effects indicate relatively poor substitutability. Thus, consumption composition will not be highly sensitive
to minor price changes since other factors are more important determinants
in allocating consumptive choices. Given greater demands in the economy
for transport inputs, under relatively inelastic behavior, we would expect
rather large shifts in transport consumption over time. This would result
only under conditions of changing technology. This is reflected in Table
24, where the large positive temporal effects are associated with the relatively inelastic pricing reactions.

If our reasoning about temporal composition effects and price elasticities is correct, then perhaps we may be able to infer the magnitude of

---

[1]If the two goods are perfect substitutes for one another then, in
theory, they are the same good--indistinguishable. Infinity elasticity
would result.

[2]Since collusion is illegal it is difficult to gather evidence to
verify its presence. Alternatively, there is quite a bit of evidence available from the transport industries about differing forms of discrimination.
These can serve to allocate transport consumption just as well as collusion. For examples, see: D. P. Locklin, Economics of Transportation (Home-
wood, Illinois: R. D. Irwin Company, 1960), especially chapters xxi, xxii,
and xxiii.

[3]Under a fixed technology.

the price elasticity for the Northwestern Region. Of the nine elasticities estimated in Table 24, the Northwest is the only one which is not significant. It displays a standard error which is larger, in absolute value, than the parameter estimates itself. The combination of inelastic estimate and exceedingly large standard error precludes reliability. But note the temporal effects in the Northwest. Of all the regions, the relative growth of the motor carriers here has been phenomenal, almost 35%. Under effective competition and substitution of modes we would expect rather small growth trends for motor carriers, as evidenced in some of the other regions. On the other hand, where the two modes are poor substitutes we would expect relatively large shifts in the composition of transport consumption over time. The Northwestern Region displays a large compositional shift over time and we, therefore, presume that the true elasticity estimate should be rather inelastic. Perhaps, then, the obtained estimate of -.485 may be more reliable than indicated in Table 24. We think so.

Table 24 indicates that all commodity coefficients in all regions have negative signs, except for some of the animal product estimates. That is, the intercepts or level of consumption for individual commodity groups by region would be less than the standard intercepts of the table. Recall that the intercepts of Table 24, equation 7.8, represent a combination of manufactures and observations in 1956, the two omitted dummy variables. All estimates in the table are measured as deviations from this combined datum. Now the temporal base, 1956, will have little influence on the level of commodity demand. Therefore, except for animal products in six regions, all commodity groups represent lower levels of relative consumption than do manufactures.

To reiterate, the commodity coefficients refer to the influence that that commodity has on the change in the consumption ratio. Since the intercept refers to the base motor carrier-rail mix for manufactures, all commodities for which railroads maintain a comparative advantage (relative to the intercept base) will display negative signs. Conversely, commodities for which motor carriers capture the major share of the market will display positive signs, if such composition represents a greater motor carrier specialization than does manufactures. Note that the highest commodity coefficients are found under Z_3, products of mines. Table 19 has indicated, already, that the railroads seem to have maintained a specialization in mine product carriage. Thus, the consumption ratio for mine products will have a negative sign relative to the consumption composition for manufactures. This is clearly visible in Table 24. The largest Z_3 coefficient values in this table pertain to the Southern, Middle Atlantic, Central,

and Northwestern Regions. These regions are exactly the same as those iso-
lated in Table 19 for mine products. They are the coal regions.

Thirty of the thirty-six commodity coefficients display negative
signs. This indicates that for most commodities the consumption mix is less
favorable for motor carriers than is the case with respect to manufactures.
Alternatively, the only commodity coefficients which display positive signs
are those for animal products. This implies that the consumption mix for
animal products is more favorable for motor carriers than the carriage of
manufactures. This occurs in sufficient degree in the Southern, Middle
Atlantic, New England, and Central Regions but only to a moderate degree in
the Southwestern and Pacific Regions. Animal products clearly indicate the
results from the interaction of a high value product, a relatively station-
ary railroad technology, provision of highways, and a superior and more
flexible motor carrier technology. Namely, an increasing share of the market is being captured by motor carriers.

One other commodity category will be examined, briefly. Notice
that for forest products, Z_2, the Southern, Northwestern, Southwestern,
Rocky Mountain, and Pacific Regions display negative signs in Table 24.
These regions are all major timber and pulp producers. The magnitudes and
signs of the important forest products regions indicate that the railroads
have retained significant market advantages. In fact, the share of the
transport market for forest products is substantially lower for motor carriers than is the case with manufactures.

These inferences from the commodity estimates about transportation
specialization have important implications. First, we are led to believe
that for bulk goods, such as mine and forest products, the railroads have
been able to retain a significant share of the total transport market.
Secondly, it is the non-bulk, high value categories in which motor carriers
have been most successful in capturing increasing market shares, such as
manufactures and animal products. This results from either technical comparative advantage, qualitative comparative advantage, or a conscious effort on the part of the motor carriers to "skim the cream" traffic and leave
the residual. No doubt all three reasons have been operative.[1]

Our analysis of equation 7.8 and the results obtained have been most
revealing, but it should be apparent that much of the explanatory power of
the model was due to the set of commodity variables. To retain compara-

---

[1] For a short discussion on the relative advantages between modes,
see: J. R. Meyer, "A Comparison of the Advantages and Disadvantages of
the Various Modes of Transport," in Technical Change and the Future of
the Railways (Evanston: The Transportation Center, 1961), pp. 1-15.

bility with our earlier analysis efforts, we shall omit the relatively redundant set of variables, time, and re-specify the model as

$$\text{Log } (Q_m/Q_r) = a + b \text{ Log } (P_m/P_r) + \sum_{k=2}^{5} f_k Z_k \qquad (7.9)$$

where the Z_k are the commodity variables. One function such as 7.9 was estimated for each region and the results are presented in Table 25.

First, note that little explanation has been lost in estimating
7.9 as compared to equation 7.8. In Table 25 all the R^2 are greater than .97;
but what has happened to the elasticity estimates? Now, only three of them
are significant and two have switched signs. Clearly, most of the explanation of 7.9 is provided by the commodity variables, of which most are significant, and little explanation is provided by pricing effects. Of all the
commodity estimates only two have switched signs from Table 24 to Table 25,
animal products in the Southwest and agriculture in the Southern Region.
This stability of signs in the commodity parameters is heartening.

The major change from equation 7.8 to 7.9 involves the elasticity
estimates. In the former specification all the signs were correct, the
relative magnitudes appeared reasonable, and eight out of nine coefficients
were significant. In the present case only three coefficients are significant and two of them are overly elastic. All non-significant estimates are
small in absolute value, but their large standard errors indicate that it is
possible the true parameter estimates have larger values.

Comparison of Tables 23, 24, and 25 reveals that we have moved from
highly elastic and unlikely estimates to moderately elastic and quite likely
estimates to highly inelastic and unlikely estimates. There seems to be
little theoretical rationale to support the former and latter sets of estimates, but there is an abundant amount of theoretical justification for
the middle set of estimates. Not only do the estimates of equation 7.8
make theoretical sense, but they also accord well with what we know of the
surface transport modes. Therefore, we shall accept the estimates of equation 7.8

Inclusion of a set of time variables in equation 7.8 explicitly ac-
counts for secular trends and a well-defined inverse demand relationship
results. This is seen quite clearly in Table 24 where meaningful elasticities
have been derived. On the other hand, equation 7.9 is estimated with commodity variables and the time variables have been omitted. That is, secular trends have not been explicitly accounted for and their influence con-
founds the elasticity estimates derived in Table 25. Thus, the inverse
demand relation obtained in equation 7.8 so clearly is poorly defined in
the model specification of equation 7.9.

TABLE 25

ESTIMATES OF EQUATION 7.9

Coefficient		Southern	Middle Atlantic	New England	Central	North Western	Mid-Western	South Western	Rocky Mountain	Pacific
Intercept	a	1.4464	1.5832	1.5965	1.6632	1.8227	1.6826	1.4511	1.5732	1.6393
Prices	b	-.1951 (.5720)	.4218 (.5167)	-1.0474** (.2624)	-.1614 (.6419)	.7851 (.5460)	-1.7787** (.3543)	-.2161 (.4104)	-1.9249** (.3559)	-.4304 (.2630)
Commodities										
z_2	f_2	-1.5948** (.3296)	-1.1097** (.2148)	-.8310** (.1745)	-.9672** (.3339)	-2.1003** (.3698)	-.4873** (.1522)	-1.5115** (.2161)	-1.5164** (.1117)	-1.5878** (.0557)
z_3	f_3	-1.5789** (.0990)	-2.3299** (.1642)	-.9988** (.1119)	-1.8020** (.1756)	-3.4467** (.5235)	-.8051** (.1619)	-.6851** (.0810)	-.7476** (.0728)	-.5936** (.0517)
z_4	f_4	.6992** (.1140)	.5179** (.0823)	.4153** (.0710)	.0998 (.0636)	-2.3833 (.1066)	-.5605** (.1006)	-.0121** (.1595)	-.1121 (.0829)	.2297** (.0510)
z_5	f_5	.6181** (.1238)	-1.1390** (.2202)	-.7195** (.0662)	-.1720** (.3103)	-2.0147** (.2115)	-.8825** (.1568)	-1.1638** (.2055)	-.5782** (.1550)	-.5840** (.0852)
Coefficient	R^2	.9849	.9856	.9848	.9896	.9866	.9883	.9707	.9816	.9874

**Significant at .01 level.

The meso analysis for regions has indicated that there is sharp diversity in the price elasticities for transport demand, given the set of regions utilized. Table 24 indicates that elasticities estimated vary from a high of -1.7164 in the Mid-Western Region to a low of -.4859 in the Northwestern Region. This implies that there is a marked diversity in the substitutability of surface transport modes in the nine regions. In the Pacific, Rocky Mountain, Midwestern, and New England Regions there seems to be effective competition between modes. On the other hand, the Southern, Middle Altantic, and Northwestern Regions indicate little substitution between modes.

The observed variability in regional price elasticities and the persistent capture by the motor carrier of larger shares of the freight market are not independent phenomena. Though there are regional differences in the growth of motor carrier market shares, this growth appears related, primarily, to mode substitutability (elasticity) between regions. Moreover, mode substitutability between regions is a function of regional specialization in production. Thus, the relative effectiveness of competition between transport modes is ultimately dependent upon a regional production mix and concomitant transport demands, from which mode substitutability is derived.

Theory indicates that where there is marked competitive behavior between two services then the consumption composition will change little in the short run, ceteris paribus. We have been able to indicate such behavior in our analysis. Where elastic estimates were obtained there have been moderate compositional shifts in consumption. Conversely, where inelasticity and poor substitutability prevail there has been a rapid shift in consumption composition. In all cases, the motor carrier is capturing larger shares of the total freight transportation market, but there is marked regional variation in the pattern of growth due to production specialization.

CHAPTER VIII

MICRO ANALYSIS--REGIONS AND COMMODITIES

We now turn to an analysis of transport demand in each region for each commodity group. Chapter vii indicated that there were significant regional variations in transport demand and that regional transport demand had a significant commodity variability component, too. This agrees with the conclusions of chapter v. Therefore, there is reason to believe that the joint variability of transport demand by region and commodity will be of some interest in spite of the results of chapter vi.[1]

Our intention is to follow the research strategy applied in the previous chapters, where initially the basic model was applied to estimate transport demand. In the present instance we are dealing with the "building blocks" of the entire study--each region and each commodity class. From these data all of the prior analyses were formulated with appropriate aggregation modifications. In the Micro Analysis there is no data aggregation; instead the basic observational units are used.[2] Recall that there are nine regions and five commodity groups with observations for each set over a five-year interval. For each region we shall estimate transport demand for each commodity group. Conceptually, then, five demand functions or sets of functions will require estimation for each region.

The Basic Model

Following the strategy of equation 4.9 we first estimated transport demand by mode as a function of its own price, such as:

$$\text{Log } Q_m = a_m + b_m \text{ Log } P_m \qquad (8.1)$$

and

$$\text{Log } Q_r = a_r + b_r \text{ Log } P_r \qquad (8.2)$$

---

[1]In chapter vi we were not able to achieve meaningful transport demand estimates by commodity classes.

[2]They are basic in the sense that they are the smallest data units available. All prior analyses are formulated in terms of these data. But reference to Data--Availability and Utility, chapter iii, will serve to indicate that the railroad series utilized required construction from a state-to-state basis.

TABLE 26

ESTIMATES OF EQUATION 8.1

	coefficient	Southern	Middle Atlantic	New England	Central	North Western	Mid-Western	South Western	Rocky Mountain	Pacific
				MANUFACTURES						
Intercept	a_m	9.795	4.177	4.097	6.665	6.457	7.937	6.927	7.465	6.261
Log P_m	b_m	-2.440*	3.535*	2.843*	.854	.434	-.994	.105	-.713*	1.021
		(.640)	(.887)	(.697)	(.829)	(.232)	(.505)	(.506)	(.203)	(.349)
Coefficient of Determination	R^2	.8288	.8411	.8472	.2612	.0124	.5631	.0141	.8035	.7401
				FORESTS						
Intercept	a_m	7.793	2.789	4.926	6.166	1.746	5.547	5.094	7.399	5.788
Log P_m	b_m	-2.255	1.730	-.369	-.983	2.487	-1.050*	-.216	-2.389*	-.292
		(1.236)	(.840)	(.706)	(1.080)	(1.342)	(.312)	(.743)	(.610)	(.342)
Coefficient of Determination	R^2	.5260	.5852	.0834	.2155	.5333	.7901	.0274	.8634	.1963
				MINES						
Intercept	a_m	6.983	7.520	5.566	6.681	5.557	6.680	6.769	5.330	6.684
Log P_m	b_m	-1.930**	-2.470**	-1.053**	-1.222	-.909	-1.855**	-.989	1.273	-1.176
		(.252)	(.429)	(.079)	(.832)	(.540)	(.316)	(.774)	(1.117)	(.882)
Coefficient of Determination	R^2	.9512	.9168	.9831	.4183	.4852	.9198	.3524	.3023	.3719
				ANIMALS						
Intercept	a_m	9.030	5.380	4.723	7.809	4.400	6.971	7.254	6.853	5.364
Log P_m	b_m	-2.219**	.4453	.3363	-1.350	1.307	-.8196	-1.281	-1.056	.1490
		(.374)	(.199)	(.810)	(.465)	(1.033)	(.736)	(.763)	(3.909)	(.500)
Coefficient of Determination	R^2	.9214	.6244	.0543	.7372	.3479	.2921	.4842	.0237	.0287
				AGRICULTURE						
Intercept	a_m	9.477	3.455	5.249	10.067	4.020	4.480	10.073	8.679	6.893
Log P_m	b_m	-3.097	1.754	-.303	-3.859	1.227	.783	-3.753	-2.572**	-.663*
		(1.075)	(2.210)	(2.454)	(2.162)	(2.061)	(.957)	(2.452)	(.265)	(.161)
Coefficient of Determination	R^2	.7342	.1735	.0050	.5151	.1054	.1824	.4376	.9690	.8484

* significant at .05 level.   ** significant at .01 level.

TABLE 27

ESTIMATES OF EQUATION 8.2

	coefficient	Southern	Middle Atlantic	New England	Central	North Western	Mid-Western	South Western	Rocky Mountain	Pacific
MANUFACTURES										
Intercept	a_r	5.760	7.564	1.292	8.277	6.252	5.300	5.395	5.591	5.593
Log P_r	b_r	- .024	-1.767	3.554	-2.296	-1.049	.073	.177	- .429	- .125
		(.472)	(2.471)	(1.511)	(1.712)	(1.305)	(.419)	(.741)	(.414)	(.563)
Coefficient of Determination	R^2	.0008	.1453	.6477	.3731	.1781	.0100	.0188	.2639	.0163
FORESTS										
Intercept	a_r	5.438	4.592	4.593	4.667	4.246	6.179	4.803	5.944	6.901
Log P_r	b_r	.1356	- .534	- .536	- .450	.378	-2.835	.393	-1.225	-1.363
		(.220)	(.765)	(1.041)	(.985)	(.898)	(2.352)	(.278)	(.480)	(.470)
Coefficient of Determination	R^2	.1117	.1396	.0806	.0650	.0558	.3251	.3995	.6844	.7366
MINES										
Intercept	a_r	6.186	5.550	4.578	6.927	6.110	5.237	5.690	4.811	5.853
Log P_r	b_r	.082	1.641	- .234	-2.733	-2.963**	.129	- .267	1.017	-1.247
		(.435)	(4.052)	(1.483)	(2.746)	(.317)	(.519)	(1.290)	(.425)	(.612)
Coefficient of Determination	R^2	.0116	.0517	.0083	.2486	.9666	.0203	.0139	.6558	.5799
ANIMALS										
Intercept	a_r	2.262	3.570	2.327	2.017	2.432	4.252	3.229	11.865	4.301
Log P_r	b_r	1.194	.150	.671	1.773	1.318	.179	.695	-5.620	- .533
		(1.167)	(.872)	(1.573)	(1.317)	(1.206)	(1.267)	(1.745)	(5.301)	(.793)
Coefficient of Determination	R^2	.2585	.0097	.0572	.3764	.2846	.0066	.0502	.2725	.1311
AGRICULTURE										
Intercept	a_r	5.014	3.572	2.815	5.476	4.061	4.895	6.200	5.307	7.061
Log P_r	b_r	- .136	1.641	1.012	- .034	1.501	.764	-1.202	- .261	-1.567
		(.193)	(.699)	(.740)	(.529)	(.590)	(2.044)	(.410)	(.291)	(1.980)
Coefficient of Determination	R^2	.1415	.6471	.3838	.0014	.6833	.0446	.7405	.2113	.1726

* significant at .01 level.

where the subscripts m and r pertain to motor carriers and railroads, respectively. In the formulation of 8.1 and 8.2 estimates are derived for each mode separately. Thus, five such demand pairs have to be estimated for each region, one pair for each commodity group. With ten functions per region and commodity group, a total of ninety demand functions must be estimated. Results are displayed in Tables 26 and 27.

For equation 8.1 the range of explanation, R^2, varied from a low of .0050 to .9831, which is the best fit. This is a phenomenal range of variation. It indicates that the simple quantity-price relation performs differentially; sometime it is clearly defined and results in much explanation, but at other times the relation is ill defined. Moreover, of the forty-five slope parameters, the b_m, only twenty-nine display negative signs, the expected inverse relationship. Almost all of the commodity groups have an approximately equal number of positive and negative coefficients, except for products of forests and mines. These two commodity classes have a predominance of negative signs. The former class, forest products, provides relatively meager explanation throughout the set of functions and only two slope parameters are significant. On the other hand, mine products has eight negative coefficients of which four are highly significant. The R^2 values range from .3719 to .9831 and the four significant functions have R^2 values greater than .900.

Equation 8.2, for railroads, provides R^2 values which vary from .0008 to .7405 and twenty-four of the slope parameters are negative. None of the commodity classes yielded similar explanatory power consistently. Rather some regions performed well on a particular commodity class, but most of the remaining commodity classes provided rather poor fits. In Table 27 approximately one region in each commodity class provided a reasonably good fit. A comparison of Tables 26 and 27 will serve to emphasize that R^2 values are appreciably higher in the former table.

Results from equation 8.1 and 8.2 leave something to be desired. For some regions and some commodity groups appreciable explanation is provided, while for other region-commodity combinations there is little resolution. It may be that there are important relations between regional specialization in production, trade or business cycles as they affect regional production, and the sensitivity of transport demand. There is little empirical data to further examine these potentially important issues.[1] For

---

[1]This author is unaware of firm output indexes or areal output indexes which are conformable with the commodity and regional classifications used in this study. Examination of the sensitivity of transport demand to regional trade or business cycles would require a more disaggregative type analysis, both in terms of commodities handled and regional structure of the economy.

the moment we shall reserve judgment on equations 8.1 and 8.2 and see
whether better resolution can be attained under alternative model specifications.

The second model specification attempted relates consumption to a
set of two prices, one for motor carriers and the other for railroads.
Thus,

$$Log \ Q_m = a_m + b_{mm} \ Log \ P_m + b_{mr} \ Log \ P_r \qquad (8.3)$$

and

$$Log \ Q_r = a_r + b_{rm} \ Log \ P_m + b_{rr} \ Log \ P_r \qquad (8.4)$$

where quantities consumed are a function of both own price and alternative
price. Results of 8.3 and 8.4 are presented in Tables 28 and 29 and they
rival those obtained from equations 8.1 and 8.2 in quality.

Equation 8.3, the motor carrier demand function, displays R^2 values
ranging from a low of .0201 to .9974 as the largest value. Again one notes
an exceedingly wide range in explanatory power. Of the forty-five own price
elasticities of equation 8.3, the b_{mm}, thirty have negative signs. Note
that products of mines have eight negative slope parameters and products
of agriculture have seven negative signs. In short, these two commodity
classes provide over one-half of all negative signs obtained and they provide rather consistently high R^2 values.

The railroad demand function, equation 8.4, has an R^2 range from
.0096 to .9753; this again is a wide range of explanation. Of the forty-
five own price elasticities, the b_{rr}, twenty-eight have negative signs.
Except for products of agriculture, which has only three negative signs,
inverse slope parameters are spread quite evenly amongst the commodity
classes. Though the over-all range of R^2 is similar for both motor carriers and railroads, the railroads yield consistently lower levels of explanation.

In the estimation of equations 8.3 and 8.4 the pattern of R^2 displays a range of variation closely approximating the complete zero-one scale.
This, of course, bodes ill. In the motor carrier function 66% of the
slope parameters had negative signs and 62% had negative signs in the railroad function. Though demand theory predicates an inverse quantity-price
relation, a negative b, our results fall short of complete verification
of that theoretical construct. Furthermore, the pattern of cross effects
is rather unstable. For the railroads approximately one-half of the cross
effects display negative signs, while 60% of the motor carrier cross effects
have negative signs. To add to our difficulty in interpretation is the

TABLE 28

ESTIMATES OF EQUATION 8.3

	coefficient	Southern	Middle Atlantic	New England	Central	North Western	Mid-Western	South Western	Rocky Mountain	Pacific
				MANUFACTURES						
Intercept	a_m	9.920	2.148	5.101	8.005	10.990	7.834	8.762	9.085	8.052
Log P_m	b_{mm}	-2.324	4.819**	2.703	.850	-.889	-1.077	-.283	-.424	.450
		(1.122)	(.468)	(.713)	(.756)	(3.759)	(1.070)	(.343)	(.144)	(.563)
Log P_r	b_{mr}	-.2668	.880	-.847	-1.306	-3.231	.198	-1.436	-1.800	-1.161
		(1.843)	(.212)	(.856)	(1.027)	(6.651)	(2.083)	(.576)	(.604)	(.940)
Coefficient of Determination	R^2	.8305	.9833	.8974	.5913	.1165	.5650	.7596	.9638	.8526
				FORESTS						
Intercept	a_m	5.906	1.129	4.932	7.219	6.448	4.076	6.583	-5.051	6.588
Log P_m	b_{mm}	.010	2.647	-.675	-1.040	.173	-.887*	-.807	.490	-.039
		(1.289)	(.872)	(.795)	(.680)	(3.013)	(.215)	(1.222)	(1.192)	(.355)
Log P_r	b_{mr}	-1.584	.749	.561	-1.547	-3.064	1.502	-1.906	7.770	-.898
		(.704)	(.455)	(.605)	(.653)	(3.534)	(.663)	(2.891)	(3.053)	(.663)
Coefficient of Determination	R^2	.8658	.8237	.3589	.7938	.6603	.9411	.2008	.9613	.5811
				MINES						
Intercept	a_m	5.731	6.534	5.829	6.761	5.809	6.775	6.887	5.308	7.031
Log P_m	b_{mm}	-3.119	-3.042*	-1.074**	-1.195	-1.375	-1.426	-.954	.224	-1.1543
		(1.154)	(.774)	(.038)	(1.054)	(1.008)	(.684)	(.985)	(1.181)	(1.058)
Log P_r	b_{mr}	4.242	2.855	-.522	-.336	1.420	-1.567	-.313	1.192	-.745
		(4.021)	(3.176)	(.156)	(3.384)	(2.441)	(2.158)	(2.500)	(.810)	(2.393)
Coefficient of Determination	R^2	.9686	.9408	.9974	.4211	.5596	.9365	.3574	.6649	.4010
				ANIMALS						
Intercept	a_m	9.189	5.529	4.609	8.546	7.276	6.123	8.592	-11.128	5.299
Log P_m	b_{mm}	-1.890*	.480	-.088	.236	.224	-.990	-1.411	-2.797	.137
		(.349)	(.203)	(1.241)	(.361)	(1.345)	(.890)	(.833)	(3.652)	(.661)
Log P_r	b_{mr}	-.541	-.183	.524	-2.263*	-1.278	.745	-1.008	14.783	.056
		(.315)	(.185)	(1.013)	(.463)	(1.064)	(1.317)	(1.278)	(10.701)	(1.243)
Coefficient of Determination	R^2	.9681	.7479	.1661	.9776	.6123	.3897	.6069	.5002	.0297
				AGRICULTURE						
Intercept	a_m	7.959	13.470	6.564	10.107	20.297	2.154	8.235	8.771	6.540
Log P_m	b_{mm}	-1.291	-5.186	-3.036	-2.782	-5.322	1.212	.348	-3.736	-.673
		(1.161)	(3.354)	(15.82)	(1.862)	(2.610)	(1.084)	(1.226)	(1.305)	(.269)
Log P_r	b_{mr}	-.762	-3.376	1.443	-1.938	-11.801	2.324	-4.045*	1.559	.291
		(.373)	(1.478)	(8.230)	(1.190)	(4.223)	(2.506)	(.854)	(1.710)	(2.078)
Coefficient of Determination	R^2	.9137	.7707	.0201	.7902	.8171	.4278	.9539	.9781	.8499

* significant at .05 level.   ** significant at .01 level.

TABLE 29

ESTIMATES OF EQUATION 8.4

	coefficient	Southern	Middle Atlantic	New England	Central	North Western	Mid- Western	South Western	Rocky Mountain	Pacific
				MANUFACTURES						
Intercept	a_r	5.775	18.445	3.598	9.650	5.547	5.029	6.300	5.621	6.462
Log P_m	b_{rm}	.5168	-8.987	-1.990	-1.268	.318	- .545	- .515	.015	- .361
		(.351)	(6.231)	(.707)	(1.263)	(1.287)	(.245)	(.485)	(.161)	(.677)
Log P_r	b_{rr}	- .633	-4.468	3.080*	-2.304	- .639	.940	- .214	- .473	- .620
		(.576)	(2.831)	(.848)	(1.714)	(2.278)	(.478)	(.815)	(.683)	(1.129)
Coefficient of Determination	R^2	.5202	.5806	.9289	.5834	.2026	.7141	.3719	.2672	.1390
				FORESTS						
Intercept	a_r	5.915	7.621	6.882	6.338	5.371	6.050	4.389	4.740	6.891
Log P_m	b_{rm}	- .500	-2.131	-2.580**	-1.366	- .256	.059	.224	.297	- .036
		(.709)	(1.781)	(.322)	(.804)	(2.316)	(.994)	(.141)	(.720)	(.362)
Log P_r	b_{rr}	.348	-1.245	.279	- .497	- .611	-2.773	.783	- .497	-1.327
		(.387)	(.930)	(.245)	(.772)	(1.971)	(3.066)	(.336)	(1.853)	(.675)
Coefficient of Determination	R^2	.2886	.4984	.9722	.6172	.0992	.3263	.7325	.7092	.7379
				MINES						
Intercept	a_r	5.661	7.931	4.366	6.409	6.138	5.226	5.599	5.094	5.924
Log P_m	b_{rm}	- .533	2.589	.208	1.463*	- .042	.425	.722	- .761	- .456*
		(.605)	(1.061)	(.428)	(.328)	(.262)	(.264)	(.406)	(.788)	(.080)
Log P_r	b_{rr}	1.898	-7.055	- .097	-3.967	-2.882*	-1.030	- .790	1.330	-1.177**
		(2.108)	(4.351)	(1.736)	(1.056)	(.636)	(.834)	(1.032)	(.538)	(.182)
Coefficient of Determination	R^2	.2882	.7610	.1134	.9312	.9671	.5728	.6175	.7652	.9753
				ANIMALS						
Intercept	a_r	.212	4.530	.636	2.225	- .928	3.493	- .093	11.961	4.293
Log P_m	b_{rm}	2.335	-1.228	3.317	1.756	1.840	1.438	1.849*	- .894	.042
		(.933)	(.812)	(2.091)	(2.587)	(2.212)	(.456)	(.560)	(2.279)	(.554)
Log P_r	b_{rr}	.034	.344	-1.116	- .250	2.324	- .541	1.255	-4.713	- .563
		(.842)	(.740)	(1.711)	(3.314)	(1.755)	(.676)	(.858)	(6.664)	(1.046)
Coefficient of Determination	R^2	.8205	.5380	.5807	.4932	.4684	.8332	.8527	.3249	.1337
				AGRICULTURE						
Intercept	a_r	6.500	-1.987	5.971	5.327	1.110	1.644	5.415	5.437	6.675
Log P_m	b_{rm}	-1.478*	4.031	-6.278	.1391	1.341	1.623*	.9335	- .9826	- .117
		(.449)	(3.581)	(8.164)	(1.076)	(.373)	(.340)	(.778)	(1.102)	(.244)
Log P_r	b_{rr}	.227	3.249	4.212	- .066	3.455*	2.370	-1.665	.997	-1.180
		(.145)	(1.580)	(4.236)	(.691)	(.605)	(.786)	(.544)	(1.444)	(2.431)
Coefficient of Determination	R^2	.8663	.7837	.5244	.0096	.9574	.9229	.8490	.4355	.2587

* significant at .05 level.   ** significant at .01 level.

fact that there is no apparent consistency in the signs of own price and cross price elasticities for any one function.

Before judging the operation of the basic model one last specification will be presented. Perhaps the inverse demand relation we are seeking is ill-defined because of demand shifts over time. Such shifts could be ascertained through the introduction of a trend term, as was done in prior chapters. If time trends could be accounted for then, perhaps, the true inverse demand relation will be more clearly defined.

In the present instance we have five observations for each commodity in each region. Introducing four dummy time variables would eliminate all available degrees of freedom.[1] Thus, we are forced to introduce time as a linear trend term, which requires only one degree of freedom. The revised specification is, therefore:

$$\text{Log } Q_m = a_m + b_{mm} \text{ Log } P_m + c_m T \qquad (8.5)$$

and

$$\text{Log } Q_r = a_r + b_{rr} \text{ Log } P_r + c_r T \qquad (8.6)$$

where m and r represent the two transport modes and T is a linear dummy variable for time.[2] A linear term such as T extracts a time trend, by definition. Thus, the coefficient estimate obtained implies a constant rate of annual change, equal to c, over the 1956-1960 interval. It is, therefore, an average type of time change. Results for equations 8.5 and 8.6 are presented in Tables 30 and 31.

Estimation of equations 8.5 and 8.6 results in improved "goodness of fit" and a noticeable but smaller improvement in the direction of coefficient signs. In almost all cases the range of explained variation for any commodity group from 8.5 and 8.6 has been substantially reduced relative to results from 8.1 through 8.4. The range of R^2 is smallest for products of mines, both for motor carriers and railroads. Conversely, the largest range pertains to forest products for both modes. Animal products evidence a rather large but constant range for both modes, while agriculture and manufactures display prominent shifts between modes. For the motor carriers, manufactures and agriculture display a modest R^2 spread. For railroads, the spread is quite marked. A small range between high

---

[1] In previous chapters dummy variables for time were added explicitly, one for each year.

[2] A linear time trend is entered as a column vector, such as 1, 2, . . . 5, where the values are allocated sequentially according to the observation year.

TABLE 30

ESTIMATES OF EQUATION 8.5

	coefficient	Southern	Middle Atlantic	New England	Central	North Western	Mid-Western	South Western	Rocky Mountain	Pacific
					MANUFACTURES					
Intercept	a_m	5.652	5.007	5.274	2.507	7.102	7.569	7.805	7.465	6.564
Log P_m	b_{mm}	1.243	2.623	1.530	4.801	- .431	- .644	- .835	- .713	.670
		(1.376)	(1.152)	(1.239)	(2.851)	(.653)	(.889)	(.523)	(.249)	(.660)
Time -- T	c_m	.081	.006	.010	- .043	.052*	.011	.024	.0005	.007
		(.029)	(.005)	(.008)	(.030)	(.008)	(.020)	(.010)	(.011)	(.010)
Coefficient of Determination	R^2	.9646	.9048	.9135	.6348	.9460	.6151	.7284	.8038	.7863
					FORESTS					
Intercept	a_m	5.603	3.173	3.715	7.324	3.332	5.547	6.129	3.998	5.923
Log P_m	b_{mm}	- .433	1.385	.819	-2.016	.999	-1.056	-1.537	- .103	- .466
		(.708)	(2.291)	(.786)	(1.093)	(.647)	(.368)	(.788)	(1.376)	(1.221)
Time -- T	c_m	.053*	.006	- .029	.041	.059*	.004	.100	.157	.004
		(.013)	(.039)	(.014)	(.025)	(.014)	(.010)	(.046)	(.089)	(.031)
Coefficient of Determination	R^2	.9431	.5910	.6883	.6550	.9504	.8063	.7089	.9361	.2054
					MINES					
Intercept	a_m	6.865	6.813	5.573	5.744	6.019	6.450	6.381	5.632	6.899
Log P_m	b_{mm}	-1.731	-1.584**	-1.057**	.196	-1.616**	-1.601	- .308	.848	-3.196
		(.591)	(.260)	(.099)	(.688)	(.199)	(1.403)	(.184)	(.522)	(1.360)
Time -- T	c_m	.012	.029*	- .002	.044	.076*	.019	.046**	- .024*	.123
		(.031)	(.006)	(.011)	(.015)	(.013)	(.104)	(.005)	(.006)	(.071)
Coefficient of Determination	R^2	.9546	.9920	.9834	.8806	.9709	.9212	.9806	.9035	.7464
					ANIMALS					
Intercept	a_m	7.839	5.614	5.997	7.966	5.109	7.095	4.586	8.804	4.939
Log P_m	b_{mm}	-1.432	.160	- .738	-1.462	.611	- .914	.474	-2.429	.486
		(.810)	(.106)	(.618)	(.967)	(.614)	(1.151)	(.205)	(1.343)	(.487)
Time -- T	c_m	.017	.016*	- .038	- .003	.019	- .003	.059**	.067*	.019
		(.016)	(.004)	(.014)	(.024)	(.006)	(.023)	(.005)	(.013)	(.013)
Coefficient of Determination	R^2	.9506	.9597	.7902	.7399	.8705	.2981	.9911	.9264	.5255
					AGRICULTURE					
Intercept	a_m	6.958	5.346	- .953	8.540	5.455	9.877	5.100	8.568	6.898
Log P_m	b_{mm}	-1.137	- .039	5.267	-2.661	- .407	-3.801	.094	-2.492	- .701*
		(1.125)	(2.221)	(2.054)	(2.846)	(.260)	(4.339)	(.799)	(.982)	(.160)
Time -- T	c_m	.051	.031	.071*	.025	.097**	.144	.107**	.003	.012
		(.022)	(.021)	(.021)	(.034)	(.006)	(.133)	(.015)	(.036)	(.011)
Coefficient of Determination	R^2	.9239	.6078	.8472	.6194	.9921	.4842	.9785	.9692	.9050

* significant at .05 level.   ** significant at .01 level.

TABLE 31

ESTIMATES OF EQUATION 8.6

	coefficient	Southern	Middle Atlantic	New England	Central	North Western	Mid-Western	South Western	Rocky Mountain	Pacific
				MANUFACTURES						
Intercept	a_r	6.201	7.654	3.548	8.110	6.895	5.892	6.516	5.424	6.599
Log P_r	b_{rr}	- .477	-1.780	1.407	-2.098	-1.629	- .543	- .894	- .284	-1.021
		(.857)	(1.107)	(1.111)	(1.383)	(.402)	(1.316)	(.594)	(.353)	(.899)
Time -- T	c_r	- .007	- .038*	- .017	- .017	- .017*	- .007	- .019	.006	- .010
		(.011)	(.010)	(.006)	(.010)	(.003)	(.015)	(.007)	(.003)	(.008)
Coefficient of Determination	R^2	.1830	.8858	.9307	.7295	.9509	.1217	.7754	.6675	.4371
				FORESTS						
Intercept	a_r	5.169	5.168	4.844	5.620	5.076	4.394	5.012	5.177	6.734
Log P_r	b_{rr}	.656	-1.140	- .829	-1.790	- .761	- .615	.018	- .494	-1.209
		(1.211)	(.452)	(.515)	(.755)	(.755)	(1.593)	(.799)	(1.586)	(.730)
Time -- T	c_r	.019	- .044	- .042*	- .049	- .033	- .037	- .010	- .019	- .003
		(.043)	(.015)	(.012)	(.018)	(.014)	(.014)	(.019)	(.040)	(.009)
Coefficient of Determination	R^2	.1901	.8407	.8559	.7951	.7434	.8500	.4691	.7185	.7501
				MINES						
Intercept	a_r	6.662	7.268	4.955	6.945	6.108	5.706	5.821	5.223	5.766
Log P_r	b_{rr}	- .952	-1.661	- .732	-2.581	-2.801**	-1.334	- .458	.315	- .959
		(.707)	(1.907)	(.259)	(1.431)	(.425)	(.438)	(.687)	(.838)	(.232)
Time -- T	c_r	- .018	- .046*	- .070**	- .031	- .007	- .039*	- .025	- .015	- .024*
		(.010)	(.012)	(.007)	(.010)	(.011)	(.010)	(.008)	(.016)	(.005)
Coefficient of Determination	R^2	.5880	.8883	.9805	.8633	.9728	.8840	.8173	.7666	.9627
				ANIMALS						
Intercept	a_r	5.556	4.514	4.481	5.496	7.076	10.114	3.815	4.673	4.446
Log P_r	b_{rr}	-1.458	- .662	-1.099	- .876*	-1.989	-3.851	.274	- .412	- .634
		(.798)	(.287)	(1.154)	(.164)	(1.071)	(1.184)	(.393)	(2.200)	(1.078)
Time -- T	c_r	- .071*	- .069*	- .085	- .068**	- .054*	- .061*	- .052**	- .035*	- .003
		(.017)	(.011)	(.033)	(.003)	(.015)	(.016)	(.006)	(.007)	(.015)
Coefficient of Determination	R^2	.9209	.9449	.7816	.9972	.9033	.8801	.9684	.9382	.1493
				AGRICULTURE						
Intercept	a_r	4.251	4.757	3.520	6.309	4.579	4.176	5.492	4.832	5.890
Log P_r	b_{rr}	5.866	.122	.426	-1.141	.905	1.576	- .374	.220	- .587
		(2.881)	(.766)	(1.324)	(.481)	(.892)	(.676)	(4.249)	(.601)	(1.608)
Time -- T	c_r	.045	- .039	- .015	- .026	- .012	.047*	.022	.015	- .019
		(.180)	(.016)	(.026)	(.009)	(.013)	(.009)	(.114)	(.017)	(.011)
Coefficient of Determination	R^2	.1679	.9094	.4710	.8039	.7764	.9340	.7454	.4470	.6788

* significant at .05 level.   ** significant at .01 level.

values, such as mine products, implies a rather good fit consistently. Conversely, large ranges imply differential applicability of the model. The model appears to perform relatively well for manufactures and agriculture with respect to motor carriers, but the same model performs less adequately for railroads, as witnessed by the R^2 range.

One additional con ideration is required before passing judgment on the estimates of equations 8.5 and 8.6. Though explanatory power may be high we should examine the signs of the estimated coefficients, both for prices and trend. Based upon our prior analyses we expect the motor carriers to have positive time coefficients, primarily, and the railroads to have negative coefficients.[1] In fact, only six of the forty-five railroad time coefficients are positive and five of the six have large standard errors. Alternatively, the motor carrier coefficients display seven negative signs and all others agree with expectations. Of the seven, all have large standard errors except mine products in the Rocky Mountain Region. Approximately 30% of the trend terms are significant for both equations 8.5 and 8.6. A comparison of Tables 30 and 31 with Tables 26 and 27 will serve to indicate the increase in R^2 values which results from trend effects. In the main, therefore, the signs of the temporal effects agree with a priori expectations and offer a large amount of increased explanation.

There has been a noticeable improvement in the price coefficients when we compare Tables 26 and 27 with Tables 30 and 31. In the former model specification twenty-nine of the motor carrier price elasticities had negative signs. In the present case there are still twenty-nine negative coefficients. With respect to railroads the number of negative coefficients was previously twenty-four and now is thirty-four. Thus, for motor carriers 64% of the price coefficients are negative and for railroads 75% are negative in the present specification.

Ideally, we would like to observe clearly defined inverse demand relations for all commodities in all regions, but then there would be little need for an extended study. With so few observations for analysis we do not expect perfect or ideal results. In spite of the lack of coefficient significance a large proportion of the price coefficients result in negative signs, as is desired. Obviously, though, the relatively large explanatory power of equations 8.5 and 8.6 has been due, primarily, to trend effects. Given the rather poor performance of equations 8.1 and 8.2 our estimates for equations 8.5 and 8.6 represent a substantial improvement. But in

---

[1]See estimates for equations 7.3, 7.4, and 7.8 for verification.

moving from the former set of equations to the latter there have been major modifications in coefficient values. We hesitate to place too much reliance upon the price elasticity estimates of equations 8.5 and 8.6 yet.

Application of the basic model has included three different specifications. First, we estimated transport demand as a function of its own price; then it was estimated as a function of own price and alternative price; lastly, demand was estimated as a function of its own price and a linear time trend. These may be represented as:

$$Q_1 = f \ (P_1)$$
$$Q_1 = f \ (P_1, P_2) \hspace{3cm} (8.7)$$
$$Q_1 = f \ (P_1, T)$$

where 1 and 2 indicate alternative transport modes. Of course, for each specification of 8.7 there is an analogous function for the second mode. The third form of the basic model, where Q is a function of P and T, was the most successful specification. It yielded the largest number of expected signs, the highest consistent set of R^2 values, and displayed the greatest amount of internal consistency of all three. Yet many of the results of equations 8.5 and 8.6 lack sufficient clarity of resolution necessary for meaningful inferences.

The Modified Model

It has become apparent that the basic model has performed with variable degrees of success. In some regions and for some commodities it performs quite adequately, but for other region-commodity combinations there is little clarity in transport demand behavior. In our efforts to find consistently more meaningful results we resort to the elasticity of substitution formulation.

In terms of the Micro Analysis the elasticity of substitution concept has an additional advantage, since fewer parameters need be estimated to express quantity-price relationships. In chapters v, vi, and vii sufficient numbers of observations were available for estimation such that degrees of freedom was not a major concern. In the present analysis only four degrees of freedom are available given five observations. Such a small number of observations places severe restrictions upon the reliability of obtained estimates,[7] especially if there is little variability in the price series

---

[1]This is amply demonstrated in the estimates for equations 8.1 through 8.6.

utilized.[1] Often, indeterminacy results in such cases.[2]

Recall that the elasticity of substitution framework is:

$$\text{Log } (Q_m/Q_r) = a + b \text{ Log } (P_m/P_r) \qquad (8.8)$$

where the relationship links quantity and price ratios. In the basic model, equations 8.3 and 8.4, the two alternative prices appeared as explicit variables and required estimates for two parameters. In 8.8 the two prices are expressed as a ratio and require only one parameter estimate to complete the linkage. With only five observations every degree of freedom saved is to our advantage. Results of estimating equation 8.8 are displayed in Table 32.

In spite of the gain in statistical efficiency of estimating 8.8 as compared to the basic model, the results obtained are exceedingly disparate. The range of R^2 in Table 32 is rather surprising. Our prior experience would indicate that the elasticity of substitution model performs more adequately than the basic model. This does not seem to be the present case. Not only is the range large, but it is uniformly large for all commodity sets and displays wide scatter within each commodity set. Such large variations in explanation cast doubt on the validity of the estimates obtained.

Under normal demand conditions we expect negative slope parameters from equation 8.8. Twenty-four functions do have negative signs, but the remaining twenty-one are positive in sign. In fact, most of the commodity groups have positive signs for most regions, except for mine and animal products. Products of mines display eight negative signs and animal products have seven negative signs, but even these functions evidence large R^2 variations. Not only is there a large range in the R^2 values in Table 32 but also the general level of explanatory power is exceedingly low, with a few exceptions. In fact, the results of 8.8 seem poorer than those derived from equations 8.1 and 8.2.

Once more one cannot help but inquire if there have been major demand shifts over time. If so, then the relatively poor explanatory power and inconsistent behavior of signs in 8.8 may be extracted. Demand shifts could arise due to a variety of conditions and they may be secular or cyclical. If secular then a time trend term will extract such shifts.

---

[1] This was discussed briefly under _Modified Basic Model_, chapter iv. It will be raised again in the latter part of this chapter.

[2] If there is absolutely no price variability then the price elasticity of demand is indeterminate. On the other hand, such conditions prove ideal for estimating income elasticities of demand.

TABLE 32

ESTIMATES OF EQUATION 8.8

	coefficient	Southern	Middle Atlantic	New England	Central	North Western	Mid-Western	South Western	Rocky Mountain	Pacific
MANUFACTURES										
Intercept	a	1.864	1.569	2.255	1.600	1.695	1.639	1.469	1.568	1.868
Log (P_m/P_r)	b	-3.175	.022	4.368**	1.022	.086	- .999	.558	- .688	.713*
		(1.369)	(2.404)	(.623)	(1.059)	(1.980)	(1.078)	(.395)	(.322)	(.157)
Coefficient of Determination	R^2	.6417	.00003	.9424	.2368	.0006	.2224	.3995	.6031	.8729
FORESTS										
Intercept	a	-1.922	.578	.084	.208	- .718	1.062	- .151	.110	.175
Log (P_m/P_r)	b	2.343*	.122	.324	.702	1.711	-1.486	- .021	-2.141*	- .007
		(.680)	(.879)	(1.103)	(.449)	(.978)	(.798)	(.655)	(.397)	(.594)
Coefficient of Determination	R^2	.7979	.0063	.0279	.4483	.5051	.5356	.0003	.9061	.00005
MINES										
Intercept	a	- .029	.487	.616	.637	- .701	1.275	.775	.713	.990
Log (P_m/P_r)	b	-2.677**	-4.720*	-1.132	-2.674	- .424	-2.600*	-1.622	.211	- .659
		(.402)	(1.173)	(.362)	(1.089)	(1.141)	(.518)	(1.156)	(.778)	(.858)
Coefficient of Determination	R^2	.9366	.8435	.7650	.6675	.0440	.8933	.3961	.0239	.1640
ANIMALS										
Intercept	a	2.451	2.134	2.005	1.979	1.960	1.051	1.821	1.454	1.974
Log (P_m/P_r)	b	-1.285	1.052	-2.021	-3.105	1.330	-2.168	-1.441	-1.871	.029
		(2.587)	(.727)	(1.206)	(3.849)	(1.125)	(.970)	(1.476)	(6.073)	(.941)
Coefficient of Determination	R^2	.0760	.4109	.4834	.1782	.3176	.6246	.2411	.0306	.0003
AGRICULTURE										
Intercept	a	.411	- .092	1.081	- .643	- .326	.107	- .865	2.882	1.007
Log (P_m/P_r)	b	1.175	1.909	2.312	.952	1.573	- .301	2.421	-6.749	- .533
		(.383)	(1.046)	(3.803)	(1.938)	(1.463)	(.793)	(1.796)	(2.594)	(.361)
Coefficient of Determination	R^2	.7580	.5260	.1096	.0743	.2781	.0459	.3771	.6929	.4209

* significant at .05 level. ** significant at .01 level.

If cyclical demand could be affected differentially according to commodities as well as regions.[1]

In an effort to examine possible demand shifts a time trend variable was introduced. Due to the small number of degrees of freedom available a linear trend term was added, which requires only one parameter estimate. By contrast, we could have adopted a model of first differences which would have incorporated the trend term in the intercept value.[2] Given only five original observations this technique would offer no appreciable advantage. It makes little difference in estimating demand whether one has five observations and three parameters to estimate or four observations and two parameters to estimate. The former alternative was chosen, which may be represented as:

$$\text{Log } (Q_m/Q_r) = a + b \text{ Log } (P_m/P_r) + c \, T \qquad (8.9)$$

where T is a linear time trend from 1956-1960. For each commodity group nine functions such as 8.9 were estimated, one for each region, or a total of forty-five demand functions. Results are indicated in Table 33.

Estimates of equation 8.9 indicate that most of the R^2 values are rather large. Of the forty-five functions estimated and tabled only seven display R^2 values less than .6000. These are evenly distributed amongst commodities, at least one appearing in each commodity set. In terms of over-all fit equation 8.9 performs rather well. Also, all the trend terms are positive except three. Positive trend terms are, of course, expected and they indicate relative market share growth of the motor carriers. The three trend parameters which are negative are small in value and display large standard errors. Twenty-one trend parameters, almost one-half of the total, are significant and all these are positive in sign.

Notice that a majority of the price elasticities are less than -1 in magnitude, indicative of inelasticity. In fact, twenty-nine price coefficients are rather inelastic and there are at least three such cases in each commodity class. There are a total of nine positive price coefficients and each commodity group has at least one. Only three elasticity estimates of the forty-five are statistically significant, but given the few degrees of freedom there is little reason to expect general significance.

---

[1]Demand sensitivity would be dependent largely upon the regional structure of the economy. Given different structural properties the trade cycle would affect regions according to their output mixes. Our inability to attack this problem in this study was commented upon previously. See p. 100, fn. 1.

[2]See Collinearity, chapter iv, for a discussion of this technique.

TABLE 33

ESTIMATES OF EQUATION 8.9

	coefficient	Southern	Middle Atlantic	New England	Central	North Western	Mid-Western	South Western	Rocky Mountain	Pacific
					MANUFACTURES					
Intercept	a	1.458	1.423	1.068	1.630	1.397	1.563	1.370	1.579	1.761
Log (P_m/P_r)	b	-.9633	-.9696	-4.0564	-.7560	-.7939	-.3926	-.5561	-.6726	.2970
		(.385)	(.399)	(6.132)	(.750)	(.452)	(1.060)	(.333)	(.384)	(.104)
Time -- T	c	.048**	.055**	.081	.032*	.068**	.021	.036*	-.005	.012*
		(.005)	(.005)	(.058)	(.009)	(.008)	(.016)	(.009)	(.014)	(.002)
Coefficient of Determination	R^2	.9900	.9825	.9705	.8793	.9674	.5861	.9265	.6282	.9895
					FORESTS					
Intercept	a	-.205	.851	.612	.830	-.257	.921	.373	-.542	.006
Log (P_m/P_r)	b	-.3124	-1.1904	-.8923	-.5806	.3811	-1.3465	-1.8732	-.6420	-.4845
		(.073)	(.281)	(1.84)	(.461)	(.176)	(.466)	(.530)	(1.06)	(.902)
Time -- T	c	.069**	.092**	.037	.051*	.086**	.038	.168*	.141	.014
		(.001)	(.013)	(.044)	(.016)	(.007)	(.014)	(.041)	(.094)	(.019)
Coefficient of Determination	R^2	.9997	.9616	.2849	.9089	.9934	.8959	.8905	.9554	.2213
					MINES					
Intercept	a	-.131	-.284	.452	-.207	-.046	.314	.635	.678	.655
Log (P_m/P_r)	b	-1.8978	-2.0666	-1.0275**	-.3679	-1.5464	-1.0079	-.6541*	2.2986	-1.4865
		(.668)	(1.193)	(.152)	(.368)	(.685)	(1.137)	(.144)	(.990)	(1.201)
Time -- T	c	.035	.067	.070	.066**	.101	.095	.067**	-.037	.066
		(.025)	(.025)	(.017)	(.005)	(.032)	(.062)	(.004)	(.015)	(.067)
Coefficient of Determination	R^2	.9674	.9660	.9729	.9900	.8346	.9503	.9949	.7504	.4383
					ANIMALS					
Intercept	a	2.279	1.754	1.917	1.551	1.280	1.012	1.086	1.301	1.978
Log (P_m/P_r)	b	-1.3060	-1.1978	-2.1766*	.4398	-.5521	-2.1358	.2268	-2.2318	.1576
		(.306)	(.512)	(.507)	(1.320)	(.634)	(.895)	(.120)	(1.065)	(1.136)
Time -- T	c	.089**	.131*	.043	.084*	.062*	.022	.107**	.099**	.013
		(.006)	(.026)	(.011)	(.014)	(.014)	(.018)	(.004)	(.010)	(.029)
Coefficient of Determination	R^2	.9913	.9561	.9393	.9504	.9291	.7870	.9976	.9801	.0908
					AGRICULTURE					
Intercept	a	.619	.379	.699	-.037	-.279	.051	.420	-.009	.909
Log (P_m/P_r)	b	.1426	.2312	-1.9395	-.4111	-.0758	-.1532	-.9149	.2181	-.6176
		(1.342)	(1.146)	(4.824)	(1.561)	(.362)	(1.919)	(.538)	(7.731)	(.313)
Time -- T	c	.053	.067	.062	.056	.117**	-.007	.086**	.083	.030
		(.065)	(.034)	(.048)	(.028)	(.014)	(.074)	(.010)	(.086)	(.021)
Coefficient of Determination	R^2	.8175	.8358	.5064	.6800	.9794	.0497	.9828	.7895	.7194

* significant at .05 level.   ** significant at .01 level.

Note the marked difference in explanatory power between equations
8.8 and 8.9. Obviously, the high degree of explanation in 8.9 is due, primarily, to the inclusion of linear trend terms, of which a majority are significant. Also notice that many of the elasticity estimates which are close
to unity approach statistical significance. As the estimates deviate from
unitary elasticity the standard errors appear to "blow up," both for positive and negative deviations.

Highly elastic estimates imply technical as well as economic substitutability. But there is little reason to accept very large elasticity
estimates when these pertain to commodity groups in which a particular mode
is thought to maintain appreciable comparative advantage. In particular,
the one area in which railroads are thought to be maintaining their traffics
is mine products. Such a condition implies a relative if not an absolute
comparative advantage. Estimates such as those for mine products in the
Middle Atlantic Region do not support concepts of market monopoly and comparative advantage. Therefore, many of the highly elastic estimates should
be viewed with considerable care. An additional reason for caution in the
interpretation of large elasticities concerns the size of the deviations.
It was previously mentioned that as estimates deviate from unitary elasticity the errors appear to increase rapidly. Given a combination of highly
elastic estimates with large standard errors it is difficult to offer meaningful interpretations.

In the "Meso Analysis by Regions" we were able to note the association between elasticity estimates and growth trends in motor carrier market
shares. This association agreed with theoretical considerations. No such
clear association is found at the micro level. The lack of correlation between trends and elasticities is due, no doubt, to poorly defined demand behavior under an exceedingly small number of observations. It is difficult
to make meaningful inferences under these conditions.

One last experiment was attempted in order to obtain more meaningful elasticity estimates. It was thought that perhaps there are certain
trend effects operating independently upon the variables in the system.
More precisely, perhaps the effects do not operate on the price and quantity ratios equally or even in the same direction. If there are differential trend effects then they may be the cause for the poor results obtained in 8.9. Obviously, their elimination from the system would clarify
the true quantity-price relationship and, thereby, permit more meaningful
estimation.

In an effort to eliminate differential trends the quantity and

price ratios of equation 8.9 were regressed separately on a linear time trend
variable. Each regression generated a set of errors or residuals which
represent variations in the ratio left unexplained by the time trend. Thus,
temporal effects have been exised from the ratios and the residuals remain.
These residuals should indicate the true quantity-price relationship more
clearly. Constants were added to the quantity and price residuals such
that the first observation of each residual set, 1956, equalled unity.
This operation, scaling of residuals, ensures that all residuals are measured relative to a common base, observational year 1956. These operations
may be represented as:

$$\text{Log } (Q_m/Q_r) = a_1 + b_1 \, T + U \qquad (8.10)$$

and

$$\text{Log } (P_m/P_r) = a_2 + b_2 \, T + V \qquad (8.11)$$

where T is a linear time trend and the U and V are error terms or residuals.
Estimation of equations 8.10 and 8.11 extracts trend effects from each of the
ratios. Then the U and V were scaled such that all residuals were measured
relative to 1956, the base year observation. Symbolically:

$$
\begin{aligned}
U_1 + k_1 &= 1.0 = U_1' \qquad\text{and}\qquad && V_1 + k_2 = 1.0 = V_1' \\
U_2 &= k_1 = \quad = && V_2 + k_2 = \quad = \\
&\cdot && \cdot \qquad\qquad\qquad\qquad (8.12) \\
&\cdot && \cdot \\
U_5 + k_1 &= \quad = U_5' && V_5 + k_2 = \quad = V_5'
\end{aligned}
$$

where the U' and V' are the scaled ratios.

Subsequent to scaling the U', the quantity residuals were regressed
upon the V', the scaled price residuals, that is:

$$U' = a + b \, V' \qquad (8.13)$$

Note that the U' and V' are expressed in the same units as equations 8.10
and 8.11 since they are merely the scaled quantity and price residuals.
Equation 8.13 was estimated for each region and each commodity group.

Estimates of equation 8.9 indicated that most of the variability
of the demand relation was due to the trend terms. The present process of
equations 8.10 and 8.13 was designed to eliminate trends. Therefore, we
expect the estimates of 8.13 to yield lower R^2 than those previously obtained. The object of the trend extraction and scaling process was to
obtain more theoretically meaningful elasticity estimates of the true

quantity-price relationship. Slightly lower R^2 values will not disturb us. Results of fitting equation 8.13 are presented in Table 34.

In most cases the R^2 values derived from equation 8.13 are rather moderate in magnitude and they compare quite favorably with many of our prior micro level results. Of course, the level of explanation is somewhat lower for 8.13 as compared to equation 8.9, but this was anticipated. More important, though, is the exceedingly close correspondance of many of the estimates in Tables 33 and 34. In fact, at least six of the point estimates in each commodity group are almost exactly the same in Tables 33 and 34 and almost all of these have negative signs. This type of confirmatory evidence supports the notion that there are secular demand shifts, in the main, and most of our region-commodity transport demand estimates behave according to ordinary conditions. Those which deviate from expectations, and there are about ten of these, apparently represent the more unique cases where cyclical shifts may predominate.[1] The high level of agreement between equations 8.9 and 8.13 lends support to the validity of the estimates obtained. In equation 8.9 the combination of rather high R^2 values, elasticity point estimates which have been confirmed under alternative specification, and meaningful temporal effects provides a complex of heartening results.

A brief comparison of Table 15 in chapter vi and Tables 33 and 34 in the present chapter would be instructive. In the former chapter we attempted to estimate transport demand by commodity group for the nation as a unit with dummy variables included for regional and temporal shifts. At the micro level demand was estimated for each commodity and region combination. Since we have some confirmatory evidence regarding elasticity estimates in Tables 33 and 34 we shall concentrate upon those estimates which are almost identical in the two tables. By taking the simple averages of all those entries in Table 34 marked with an #, according to commodity groups, the means are derived as shown in Table 35.

Now compare the results of Table 35 with the elasticity estimates of Table 15. There is a rather close correspondance between all commodity classes except animal products. This is not particularly surprising since the aggregate model by commodities yields an elasticity estimate which reflects the national response pattern. Table 35 merely averages most of the components of that national pattern and, therefore, we should expect reasonably good correspondance. Recall, however, that this correspondance is obtained in spite of the non-significance of the elasticity estimates at

---

[1]It was not possible in this study to examine the sensitivity of transport demand to cyclical shifts in region-commodity combinations.

TABLE 34

ESTIMATES OF EQUATION 8.13

	coefficient	Southern	Middle Atlantic	New England	Central	North Western	Mid-Western	South Western	Rocky Mountain	Pacific
				MANUFACTURES						
Intercept	a	1.962	1.964	-5.940	- .419	1.772	1.409	1.545	1.656	.924
V'	b	- .963#	- .969#	6.957	1.457*	- .794#	- .392#	- .556#	- .672#	.076
		(.314)	(.326)	(2.546)	(.273)	(.369)	(.870)	(.277)	(.314)	(.051)
Coefficient of Determination	R^2	.7576	.7461	.7278	.9042	.6067	.6354	.5730	.6046	.4174
				FORESTS						
Intercept	a	1.313	- .191	1.899	1.561	.666	2.339	2.911	1.702	1.473
V'	b	- .312*#	1.346*	- .892#	- .581#	.323**	-1.346*#	-1.873*#	- .642#	- .484#
		(.060)	(.288)	(1.505)	(.376)	(.027)	(.380)	(.433)	(.867)	(.736)
Coefficient of Determination	R^2	.8997	.8788	.1047	.4419	.9785	.8066	.8617	.1545	.1260
				MINES						
Intercept	a	2.898	3.077	.492	1.375	2.585	1.970	1.658	.233	2.411
V'	b	-1.897*#	-2.067#	.270	- .368#	-1.546#	-1.008#	- .654*#	.763	-1.486#
		(.545)	(.974)	(.335)	(.301)	(.559)	(.929)	(.118)	(.334)	(.981)
Coefficient of Determination	R^2	.8012	.6001	.1772	.3319	.7179	.2818	.9109	.6339	.4334
				ANIMALS						
Intercept	a	- .978	2.202	3.161	-1.681	1.556	3.152	.782	-2.500	.793
V'	b	2.064*	-1.197#	-2.176*#	2.683*	- .552#	-2.135#	.226#	3.427	.157#
		(.551)	(.418)	(.414)	(.491)	(.518)	(.731)	(.098)	(1.737)	(.927)
Coefficient of Determination	R^2	.8236	.7318	.9018	.9086	.2743	.7398	.6395	.5647	.0095
				AGRICULTURE						
Intercept	a	-2.049	- .059	2.991	1.345	1.054	1.225	1.902	.781	1.615
V'	b	3.058**	1.075**	-1.938#	- .411#	- .076#	- .153#	- .915#	.215#	- .618#
		(.342)	(.143)	(3.938)	(1.275)	(.296)	(1.566)	(.439)	(6.307)	(.256)
Coefficient of Determination	R^2	.9639	.9493	.0747	.0334	.0214	.0031	.5907	.0003	.6604

* significant at .05 level.   ** significant at .01 level.   # almost identical with point estimates of Table 33.

TABLE 35

MEANS OF ESTIMATES CONFIRMED BY EQUATION 8.13

Commodity Class	Mean Value
Manufactures	-.7246
Forests	-.8759
Mines	-1.2896
Animals	-.9465
Agriculture	-.5562

the micro level. This type of evidence helps confirm some of our estimates, both in chapters vi and viii.

Estimation of the basic and modified models in the Micro Analysis has resulted in a large set of results, most of which are disappointing. The most meaningful sets of estimates were obtained from equations 8.9 and 8.13 and many of these estimates were almost identical. That is, they tend to confirm one another. Yet, even the best set of estimates, equation 8.9, yielded large standard errors with the point estimates obtained. Under such conditions it is difficult to make incisive inferences about motor carrier-railroad competition since the true parameter value is limited by a broad confidence region. Though our results have theoretical meaning and evidence some verification the lack of statistical significance makes generalization difficult.

Three considerations appear responsible, primarily, for the variable character of results obtained in this chapter. The first is completely statistical in nature, the second is behavioral, and the third pertains to regionalization and available data. All model specifications in this chapter operated under five observations. So few degrees of freedom are exceedingly restrictive in any analysis. Given such a small number of observations our expectations threshold was set rather low. Nonetheless, we had hoped that elasticity estimates obtained would display the expected inverse demand relationship and that some of them would be significant. Even lacking significance, similar point estimates of a likely magnitude for commodity-region combinations would have provided sufficient rationale for grouping. Then re-estimation would have been possible with at least twice as many degrees of freedom available. These expectations were not realized. Not only did the point estimates display a rather wide range but also the many positive signs precluded any sound basis for grouping.

The second restrictive element involves the lack of sufficient clarity in the data required to extract meaningful quantity-price relationships. This lack of clarity pertains to the price series utilized, in the main. The regulated nature of the transportation modes analyzed and the common practice of "umbrella pricing" policies results in rather rigid sets of prices over the short run. These do not change drastically nor do they provide sufficient variability over the five years to account for the distribution of market shares in surface transportation. The expected inverse demand relation lacks sufficient variability and clarity for significant estimation. Minor price and/or quantity alterations generate a pattern of shifts which often approximate a supply function instead of a demand function. Therefore, we obtain many positive price elasticity estimates.[1]

Thirdly, the Micro Analysis operates under a set of fixed regions, statistical areas, and a rather heterogeneous commodity classification. Both the commodity and regional classifications are somewhat arbitrary, in many respects, and they may or may not be particularly meaningful. If the regions and/or commodity classes do not define separate markets then bias is being introduced into the system. This regional-commodity units question is not independent; it is intertwined with the statistical and behavioral problems previously cited.

Given sufficient numbers of observations then theoretically meaningful estimation can be effectuated, as witnessed by chapters v, vi, and vii. In its absence the quality and reliability of results decreases, as seen in chapter viii. It is not possible in this study to determine whether the quality of results derived from the Micro Analysis are due to the regional and commodity classifications, lack of sufficient clarity in demand behavior, or a small number of available observations. We suspect all three are operative to some degree. Further research into these three suggested problem areas would help indicate the amount of interaction operating in the system. It would shed some understanding on the differential response mechanisms and their sensitivities for freight transportation and indicate whether cyclical behavior characterizes the cases for which we have generated relatively poor results.

---

[1]Supply shifts in the absence of demand shifts provide the ideal situation for demand estimation. Our problem seems to be the converse.

CHAPTER IX

CONCLUSION

This study has been concerned with the demand for freight transportation in the United States as exemplified by motor carrier and railroad behavior over the 1956-1960 interval. The primary objective has been to ascer-
tain the determinants of transport demand and estimate their influences through
the use of demand theory for different commodities and regions at several
levels of analysis. Two single equation demand models were formulated with
several modifications of each. All model specifications were estimated at
three levels of analysis: (1) aggregate transport demand for all commodities
for the entire nation (continental), (2) transport demand for the nation by
individual commodities, (3) regional transport demand for all commodities,[1]
and (4) individual region-commodity combinations.

Results

The major findings are summarized in order of their appearance in the
study rather than in order of importance.

Macro Analysis

When all commodities are grouped together in a single national demand
function it is apparent that there has been a persistent increase in motor
carrier tonnages and a smaller but obvious decrease in railroad tonnages.
This combination results in a division of the commodity transport market
such that the motor carrier fraction has been increasing in a linear fashion
at 6% per year, approximately. One might think that this consumption shift
is due to pricing policies; however, the division of market shares for all
goods does not appear to be particularly responsive to the price ratio. In
fact, the elasticity of intermodal substitution appears to approximate -1.
This means that a 10% shift in the motor carrier-railroad price ratio will
elicit a 10% shift (inverse) in the consumption ratio, or the elasticity of
substitution is unitary. Hence, the steady increase in motor carrier market

---

[1] In the study both the commodity and regional analyses (2 and 3 above)
were called meso analyses. For clarification purposes, a four-level sequence
is presented here.

shares is not due, primarily, to pricing considerations. Furthermore, national aggregate demand has significant commodity and regional variability components, as was to be expected. That is, the level of demand varied according to commodity groups. Ranked from highest to lowest they are: animals and products, manufactures, agricultural products, products of forests, and products of mines. Though the regional component was not as clear as the commodity component, its variability was apparent, nonetheless. It is suggested that perhaps these variability components are more important determinants of transport consumption composition than are market prices.

Meso Analysis--Commodities

In the linear demand model where prices for both motor carriers and railroads appear explicitly our estimates indicated that motor carrier demand was somewhat elastic for forest and mine products, mildly inelastic for manufactures and products of agriculture, and highly inelastic for animal products. For the railroads mine products appear to be slightly elastic. Statistical problems prevented us from obtaining meaningful estimates for other commodity groups in terms of railroad demand. Once again, estimates indicate that motor carriers have increased their traffic tonnages of each of the commodity groups over time while railroad consumption has declined for all categories. The modified model, the elasticity of intermodal substitution, indicates that forest and mine products have elastic responses, manufactures are mildly inelastic, and animal and agricultural products are rather inelastic. These findings are in accord, generally, with those of the previous linear model. Theory indicates that low valued commodities are extremely sensitive to minor pricing variations. Thus, bulk goods, such as mine and forest products should generate elastic estimates. Conversely, high valued goods are relatively insensitive to small price variations and, hence, manufactures should be rather inelastic. Our estimates accord with these theoretical expectations.

The market share captured by the motor carriers has been increasing rather rapidly for all commodity groups. Estimates indicate growth rates such as 15% for manufactures and between 20% and 30% for all other commodity groups relative to 1956. These shifting market share compositions are seen to be generated by differential growth and decline rates of the respective modes. For manufactures, motor carrier increases are equal, approximately, to railroad decreases (7.5%). Forest, mine, and animal products indicate approximate equal increases and decreases, too, but at higher rates (about 12%). The compositional shift for agricultural products, however, is due almost solely to motor carrier increases (some 22%) rather than railroad de-

creases (about 4%). Thus, the national growth rate (some 25%) of motor carrier relative to railroad composition for all goods is composed of differential rates based upon commodity differences. Apparently, the competition for
high valued traffics such as manufactures, which is the most profitable commodity class, has limited the motor carrier growth rate. This speaks well
for the railroads' ability to retain high value traffic. Moreover, the market
capture trends for motor carriers display marked non-linearities, and all of
the estimated commodity models indicate significant regional variability.

Meso Analysis--Regions

With respect to motor carriers it appears that the Southern, New
England, Northwestern, Midwestern, Rocky Mountain, and Pacific Regions display
slightly elastic pricing behavior. This is derived from the linear model
where all prices appear explicitly. Mild inelasticity is observed in the
Central and Southwestern Regions, and appreciable inelasticity in the Middle
Atlantic Region. For the railroads the price elasticities are inconclusive,
except for the Southwestern and Pacific Regions which display slightly elastic
responses. Since the alternative price estimates are erratic one cannot
specify whether motor carriers and railroads are economic substitutes.

The elasticity of substitution model, a more reliable specification,
indicated elastic responses in the New England, Midwestern, Rocky Mountain,
and Pacific Regions; appreciable inelasticity in the Southern, Middle Atlantic,
and Northwestern Regions, and mild inelasticity in the Central and Southwestern Regions. At the same time rather large growth rates are observable
for the motor carrier-railroad consumption ratio, indicative of commodity
market capture by the motor carriers. A growth rate of 15% characterizes
the Midwestern and Pacific Regions while growth rates of 20% to 30% characterize all other regions. No doubt these rates are due to regional productivity
mixes. In the New England and Central Regions marked railroad declines are
contributory; marked motor carrier increases are observed in Northwestern
and Rocky Mountain Regions; and both motor carrier increases and railroad
decreases are seen in the Southern, Middle Atlantic, Midwestern, Southwestern,
and Pacific Regions.

One of the major observations concerns the association between growth
rates and elasticities. Small growth rates and elastic estimates are highly
correlated. Elastic estimates indicate marked consumption compositional shifts
under minor pricing alterations. Under such conditions there appears to be
effective competition between modes. In order to maintain a share of the
market each mode must refrain from pricing itself out of the market under
elastic conditions. Thus, market share growth is limited for the motor

carriers when the elasticity of intermodal substitution is greater than -1, in absolute value. Conversely, inelastic estimates imply relatively unresponsive reactions to minor price alterations. Presumably, non-price determinants become more important for growth considerations under these conditions. In all model specifications there appears to be an appreciable commodity variability component. This implies that there may be important differential demand conditions within each region and for each commodity group.

Micro Analysis--Regions and Commodities

Our efforts met with much less success at the micro level. Several model specifications were estimated and under most specifications the reliability of obtained estimates was low. Nevertheless, the persistent motor carrier growth and railroad decline trends were observable with relative precision. They apply to almost all regions and most commodity groups within regions. Though many of the elasticity estimates were quite unreliable they indicated that much variability exists amongst the region-commodity combinations. Since there is regional specialization in production one would expect regional transport demand elasticities to reflect their distinctive productive mixes. This is apparent from our results, but the estimates derived lack the precision necessary on which to base general conclusions.

Three major considerations appear responsible for the relative unreliability of results on the individual region and commodity level. First, all the micro estimates were based on five observations. Thus, available degrees of freedom are minimal, sampling variabilities are enhanced, and reliable point estimates are not expected. Secondly, there is an apparent lack of clarity in the quantity-price relationships on the individual region-commodity basis. With many observations it is possible to extract certain extraneous effects. Under present conditions the observations are not available for such statistical usage. Additionally, little variation in the price series utilized, which is common for regulated industries, constrains effective estimation. Lastly, a fixed set of regions and a heterogeneous commodity classification were utilized. If the regions and/or commodity classes do not define separate markets then bias will be introduced in the estimation process. These three problems are interdependent and to some degree it is thought all three are operative in the system. Therefore, estimates are confounded.

Motivation

In many respects this study is unfinished. At aggregative levels of analysis meaningful results were obtained, but the more disaggregative analyses, primarily the micro level, generate highly variable results.

This is not uncommon in empirical research and essentially it pertains to
the scale of analysis. Usually, few parameters are required to describe and
explain the behavior of large groups or classes while many more parameters
are needed to describe individual behavior. This is true because the error
or probabilistic component becomes more pervasive as the group size under
analysis decreases. Some readers may feel the scale of analysis was too
broad, the regional classification was non-meaningful, or the commodity
grouping was too heterogeneous.[1] In some measure all of these potential
objections have some validity and, therefore, this study is unfinished.
Then again, it was not designed to be "definitive." On the other hand,
all studies have to end and we have chosen to terminate this study with
our poorest results.

Substantitive as well as methodological considerations served as
the stimulus for starting this research. The substantive issues were discussed in the Introduction. They rest largely upon the concept that demand
elasticities and consumption for regions and commodities has important meaning for the formulation of transportation policy. Whether results contained
in this volume can aid policy formulation for the transportation modes I
leave for others to judge. At least, this effort will add to the stock of
available information and perhaps offer some new directives for further research.

Methodologically, it seemed to me that little precise estimation is
being generated for non-metropolitan transportation studies, in spite of a
body of transportation theory, much discussion, and public concern. Therefore, the research was designed with estimation as the major objective. The
models formulated in this study and the methods used in fitting these models
are well known and quite elementary, yet a large number of readers will not
have seen these techniques before. For this group the methods used will
serve a pedagogical purpose. Throughout this research many models were
fitted which generated relatively poor results. The essence of the argument
and theory did not require such faithful reporting of results. Nevertheless, all estimates have been reported, the few good and the many poor for
three reasons. First, those readers unfamiliar with demand theory and the
estimation methods utilized should receive the benefit of complete intel-

---

[1]Such criticisms will, no doubt, reflect the focus of the respective disciplines. For example, some geographers will complain about the
scale of analysis as well as the regional classification. On the other hand,
economists are likely to concentrate about the definition and grouping of
commodities or, less likely, the delimitation of meaningful productive regions. At no time during the course of analysis did placation concern us.
Rather the emphasis has been upon a meaningful, soundly based analysis
within the constraints of available information.

lectual honesty; thus, they should learn to improve upon this study. Secondly, those persons interested in related research can compare their results with those obtained in this study and, thereby, further the development of more meaningful demand models. Thirdly, among a large part of the social science community there is little distinction drawn between prediction and estimation. This study presents ample evidence of high explanatory and predictive power through the use of relatively simple single equation models. Yet many of the estimates obtained from such models are discarded or viewed with suspicion since the criteria required for successful estimation have not been met.

Implications

Given the data used in this study we have endeavored to extract as much information as is possible from them. The results indicate marked differentials in transport demand by commodities and regions at all levels of analysis. Ultimately, we would like to examine transport demand as it relates to regional specialization in production. In the limit this would imply analysis by firm. More germane for policy purposes would be both cross sectional and time series studies of clearly defined commodities in the context of meaningful regional specializations, but such analyses are impossible given existing data sources.

Throughout this study regional, temporal, and commodity effects were ascertained through the use of dummy variables. Many such effects were significant, indicating important differences. Implicit in such a finding is the potential denial of a national transportation market. It seems more likely that a set of regional transport markets exists within a national transport market, where the characteristics of each of the subsets are intimately related to regional economic structure and output mix. This study has verified the existence of regional, temporal, and commodity effects but it has not investigated the causes of such effects. Of course, the why of it is the more challenging question and appears to be a logical next step for research. This will require the delimitation of finer commodity and regional classes, the internal homogeneity of which would be well founded rather than assumed.

A related issue concerns the independence of regional, temporal, and commodity effects. Whether they operate independently or not has not been investigated, though it is thought some interaction is present in the system. If interaction exists then it would be worthwhile to examine what effect such interaction has upon estimates. Not only would this avenue of research clarify some topics about potentially biased estimates but also it would

enter the field of regional trade and business cycles. The causality issues
in regional production and transportation demand require more disaggregative
data.

In chapter iv we discussed the variables that were used in this study.
One of the difficulties encountered in this research relates to the measurement of output and transport service cost. It was acknowledged that ton-
miles is a better output measure than tons, but no such measure was available
for motor carriers by commodity and region. Therefore, tons was utilized in
the analysis to maintain comparability between modes. Though a high correlation exists between ton-miles and tons on the national level, probably the
relationship is quite variable on an individual commodity and regional basis.
An additional difficulty relates to the measurement of transport prices. Total
freight revenues are the only price data available for the modes. We have used
revenue per ton (deflated) as a surrogate for price in this analysis. Yet
total revenue depends upon both the tonnage and distance components. Thus,
our price measure has a distance component built into it while our output
measure does not.

Assume for the moment that there was no price variability at all in
a given region for a given commodity class over the five-year analysis period.
Would demand estimation be possible? Theoretically, price elasticities would
be indeterminate. However, tonnages shipped would not necessarily remain
constant. The composition of regional transport shipments and distances hauled
for such shipments could be variable for an aggregate commodity class in spite
of fixed total freight revenues, because of relative changes among the different commodities making up the aggregate. In fact, demand conditions could be
changing in spite of a fixed set of prices. Thus, there is the possibility
that we have obtained pseudo demand elasticities. This type of condition becomes more acute when one deals with regulated industries such as transportation. Sufficient price variability exists in the data used so that we are
not overly concerned in our analysis about a situation as described above.
Yet price variability under few observations, as in chapter viii, is not sufficiently clear to generate reliable estimates. Resolution of this problem
can only be expected by further commodity disaggregation and the introduction
of a distance component in transportation output.

Lastly, there is the entire question of non-price determinants for
transportation demand. This area has not been considered in the present
study explicitly. Only as the non-quantifiable service features enter the
price system are they brought under analysis. Even then, however, they are
masked. Thus, service features have eluded explicit treatment.

It appears that this study has generated more questions than it has answered. Moreover, the questions generated point in the direction of more disaggregative data and analysis. In spite of severe data limitations in the transportation field[1] there are many surrogates which can be utilized at micro levels of analysis. Though the suggestions contained herein for further research will require more complicated models, presumably they will be more reliable and may be more realistic. In this fashion we shall be able to integrate regional economic specialization and derived transportation demand.

---

[1]Hopefully, additional data in the transportation field will become available soon when a census of transportation becomes a reality. There are strong indications that such a census is imminent.

SELECTED BIBLIOGRAPHY

Books

Alonso, W. Location and Land Use. Cambridge: Harvard University Press, 1964.

Barger, H. The Transportation Industries, 1889-1946. New York: National Bureau of Economic Research, 1951.

Baumol, W. J. Economic Theory and Operations Analysis. Englewood Cliffs: Prentice-Hall, 1961.

Berry, B. J. L. and Pred, A. Central Place Studies: A Bibliography of Theory and Applications. Philadelphia: Regional Science Research Institute, 1961.

Duncan, O. D. et al. Statistical Geography. Glencoe: The Free Press, 1961.

Foote, R. J. Analytical Tools for Studying Demand and Price Structures. Agriculture Handbook Number 146. Washington: U.S. Department of Agriculture, 1958.

Fisher, F. M. A Priori Information and Time Series Analysis: Essays in Economic Theory and Measurement. Amsterdam: North Holland Publishing Company, 1962.

_____. A Study in Econometrics: The Demand for Electricity in the United States. Amsterdam: North Holland Publishing Company, 1962.

Garrison, W. L., Berry, B. J. L., et al. Studies of Highway Development and Geographic Change. Seattle: University of Washington Press, 1959.

Gould, P. R. The Development of the Transportation Pattern in Ghana. Evanston: Northwestern University, Studies in Geography, Number 5, 1960.

Harberger, A. C. (ed.). The Demand for Durable Goods. Chicago: University of Chicago Press, 1960.

Hoover, E. M. The Location of Economic Activity. New York: McGraw-Hill, 1948.

Isard, W. Location and Space-Economy. Cambridge: The Technology Press and New York: John Wiley, 1956.

_____. Methods of Regional Analysis. Cambridge: The Technology Press and New York: John Wiley, 1960.

Johnston, J. Econometric Methods. New York: McGraw-Hill, 1963.

127

Kansky, K. J. Structure of Transportation Networks. Chicago: University of Chicago, Department of Geography, Research Paper No. 84, 1963.

Kindleberger, C. P. Economic Development. New York: McGraw-Hill, 1958.

Klein, L. R. An Introduction to Econometrics. Englewood Cliffs: Prentice-Hall, 1962.

Leftwich, R. H. The Price System and Resource Allocation. New York: Holt, Rinehart, and Winston, 1961.

Meyer, J. R., Peck, M. J., et al. The Economics of Competition in the Transportation Industries. Cambridge: Harvard University Press, 1960.

Nelson, R. S. and Johnson, E. M. (eds.). Technological Change and the Future of the Railways. Evanston: The Transportation Center, 1961.

Oi, W. Y. and Shuldiner, P. W. An Analysis of Urban Travel Demands. Evanston: Northwestern University Press, 1962.

Pitts, F. R. (ed.). Urban Systems and Economic Development. Eugene, Oregon: University of Oregon, School of Business Administration, 1962.

Reinsburg, M. (ed.). Private and Unregulated Carriage. Evanston: The Transportation Center, 1963.

Wold, H. and Jureen, L. Demand Analysis. New York: John Wiley, 1953.

Articles and Unpublished Materials

Alexander, D. and Moses, L. "Competition under Uneven Regulation," American Economic Review, LIII (May, 1963), 466-474.

Benishay, H. and Whitaker, G. R. "Effects of Differential Taxation on the Various Modes of Transportation: Part I, Demand for Freight Transportation," Paper read before the Econometric Society, Summer 1963.

Berry, B. J. L. "A Method for deriving Multi-Factor Uniform Regions," Przeglad Geograficzny (Polish Geographical Review), XXXIII, No. 2 (1961), 263-279.

Demsetz, H. "The Effects of Consumer Experience on Brand Loyalty and the Structure of Market Demand," Econometrica, XXX (January, 1962), 22-33.

Ferguson, C. E. and Polasek, M. "The Elasticity of Import Demand for Raw Apparel Wool in the United States," Econometrica, XXX (October, 1962), 670-699.

Harberger, A. C. "Some Evidence on the International Price Mechanism," Journal of Political Economy, LXV (December, 1957), 506-521.

Horowitz, I. "An Econometric Analysis of Supply and Demand in the Synthetic Rubber Industry," International Economic Review, IV (September, 1963), 325-345.

Kemp, M. C. "Errors of Measurement and Bias in Estimates of Import Demand Parameters," Economic Record, XXXVIII (September, 1962), 369-373.

Koutsoyannis, A. P. "Demand Functions for Tobacco," The Manchester School of Economic and Social Studies, XXXI (January, 1963), 1-19.

Kurz, M. and Manne, A. S. "Engineering Estimates of Capital-Labor Substitution in Metal Machining," American Economic Review, LIII (September, 1963), 662-679.

Meyer, J. R. "A Comparison of the Advantages and Disadvantages of the Various Modes of Transport," in Nelson, R. S. and Johnson, E. M. (eds.). Technological Change and the Future of the Railways. Evanston: The Transportation Center, 1961.

Morrill, R. L. and Garrison, W. L. "Projections of Inter-regional Patterns of Trade in Wheat and Flour," Economic Geography, XXXVI (April, 1960), 116-126.

Orcutt, G. H. "Measurement of Price Elasticities in International Trade," Review of Economics and Statistics, XXXII (May, 1950), 117-132.

Perle, E. D. "Time Series Analysis of Transportation Development: A Pilot Study of the Demand for Transportation in the United States," A report submitted to the U. S. Army Transportation Research Command by the Transportation Center at Northwestern University under contract: DA-44-177-TC-685, October 1962.

_____. "The Demand for Transportation: A Comparative View," A report submitted to the U. S. Army Transportation Research Command by the Transportation Center at Northwestern University under contract: DA-44-177-TC-685, November, 1963.

Reid, M. G. "Consumer Response to the Relative Price of Store Versus Delivered Milk," Journal of Political Economy, LXXI (April, 1963), 180-186.

Roberts, M. J. "Maximum Freight Rate Regulation and Railroad Earnings Control," Land Economics, XXXV (1959), 125-138.

Suits, D. B. "Use of Dummy Variables in Regression Equations," Journal of the American Statistical Association, LIV (December, 1957), 548-551.

Taylor, G. W. "Meat Consumption in Australia," Economic Record, XXXIX (March, 1963), 81-87.

Wilson, G. W. "On the Output Unit in Transportation," Land Economics, XXXV (August, 1959), 266-276.

Zelder, R. E. "The Elasticity of Demand for Exports, 1921-1938." Unpublished Ph.D. dissertation, Department of Economics, University of Chicago, September, 1955.

Statistical Materials

U.S. Department of Commerce, Office of Business Economics. Survey of Current Business, July, 1961.

U.S. Interstate Commerce Commission. Carload Waybill Analyses, State-to-State Distribution, Animals and Products, Traffic and Revenue. Statement Number SS-3. Annual 1956-1960.

_____. Carload Waybill Analyses, State-to-State Distribution, Manufactures and Miscellaneous, and Forwarder Traffic (c.l.), Traffic and Revenue. Statement Number SS-6. Annual 1956-1960.

_____. Carload Waybill Analyses, State-to-State Distribution, Products of Agriculture, Traffic and Revenue. Statement Number SS-2. Annual 1956-1960.

_____. Carload Waybill Analyses, State-to-State Distribution, Products of Forests, Traffic and Revenue. Statement Number SS-5. Annual 1956-1960.

_____. Carload Waybill Analyses, State-to-State Distribution, Products of Mines, Traffic and Revenue. Statement Number SS-4. Annual 1956-1960.

_____. Carload Waybill Statistics, Their History and Use. Statement Number 543. February 1954.

_____. Freight Commodity Statistics: Class I Railroads in the United States. Annual 1956-1960.

_____. Intercity Ton-Miles, 1939-1959. Statement Number 6103. April, 1961.

_____. Motor Carrier Freight Commodity Statistics: Class I Common and Contract Carriers of Property. Annual, 1956-1960.

_____. Transport Statistics in the United States: Part 7, Motor Carriers. Annual 1956-1960.

_____. Transport Statistics in the United States: Part 1, Railroads. Annual 1956-1960.

_____. Truck Traffic on Main Rural Roads, 1955. Statement Number 5710. July, 1957.

THE UNIVERSITY OF CHICAGO
DEPARTMENT OF GEOGRAPHY
RESEARCH PAPERS (Planographed, 6 × 9 Inches)

(*Available from Department of Geography, Rosenwald Hall, The University of Chicago, Chicago, Illinois, 60637. Price: four dollars each; by series subscription, three dollars each.*)

*1. GROSS, HERBERT HENRY. *Educational Land Use in the River Forest–Oak Park Community (Illinois)*
*2. EISEN, EDNA E. *Educational Land Use in Lake County, Ohio*
*3. WEIGEND, GUIDO GUSTAV. *The Cultural Pattern of South Tyrol (Italy)*
*4. NELSON, HOWARD JOSEPH, *The Livelihood Structure of Des Moines, Iowa*
*5. MATTHEWS, JAMES SWINTON. *Expressions of Urbanism in the Sequent Occupance of Northeastern Ohio*
*6. GINSBURG, NORTON SYDNEY. *Japanese Prewar Trade and Shipping in the Oriental Triangle*
*7. KEMLER, JOHN H. *The Struggle for Wolfram in the Iberian Peninsula, June, 1942—June, 1944: A Study in Political and Economic Geography in Wartime*
*8. PHILBRICK, ALLEN K. *The Geography of Education in the Winnetka and Bridgeport Communities of Metropolitan Chicago*
*9. BRADLEY, VIRGINIA. *Functional Patterns in the Guadalupe Counties of the Edwards Plateau*
*10. HARRIS, CHAUNCY D., and FELLMANN, JEROME DONALD. *A Union List of Geographical Serials*
*11. DE MEIRLEIR, MARCEL J. *Manufactural Occupance in the West Central Area of Chicago*
*12. FELLMANN, JEROME DONALD. *Truck Transportation Patterns of Chicago*
*13. HOTCHKISS, WESLEY AKIN. *Areal Pattern of Religious Institutions in Cincinnati*
*14. HARPER, ROBERT ALEXANDER. *Recreational Occupance of the Moraine Lake Region of Northeastern Illinois and Southeastern Wisconsin*
*15. WHEELER, JESSE HARRISON, JR. *Land Use in Greenbrier County, West Virginia*
*16. MCGAUGH, MAURICE EDRON. *The Settlement of the Saginaw Basin*
*17. WATTERSON, ARTHUR WELDON. *Economy and Land Use Patterns of McLean County, Illinois*
*18. HORBALY, WILLIAM. *Agricultural Conditions in Czechoslovakia, 1950*
*19. GUEST, BUDDY ROSS. *Resource Use and Associated Problems in the Upper Cimarron Area*
*20. SORENSEN, CLARENCE WOODROW. *The Internal Structure of the Springfield, Illinois, Urbanized Area*
*21. MUNGER, EDWIN S. *Relational Patterns of Kampala, Uganda*
*22. KHALAF, JASSIM M. *The Water Resources of the Lower Colorado River Basin*
*23. GULICK, LUTHER H. *Rural Occupance in Utuado and Jayuya Municipios, Puerto Rico*
*24. TAAFFE, EDWARD JAMES. *The Air Passenger Hinterland of Chicago*
*25. KRAUSE, ANNEMARIE ELISABETH. *Mennonite Settlement in the Paraguayan Chaco*
*26. HAMMING, EDWARD. *The Port of Milwaukee*
*27. CRAMER, ROBERT ELI. *Manufacturing Structure of the Cicero District, Metropolitan Chicago*
*28. PIERSON, WILLIAM H. *The Geography of the Bellingham Lowland, Washington*
*29. WHITE, GILBERT F. *Human Adjustment to Floods: A Geographical Approach to the Flood Problem in the United States*
30. OSBORN, DAVID G. *Geographical Features of the Automation of Industry* 1953. 120 pp.
*31. THOMAN, RICHARD S. *The Changing Occupance Pattern of the Tri-State Area, Missouri, Kansas, and Oklahoma*
*32. ERICKSEN, SHELDON D. *Occupance in the Upper Deschutes Basin, Oregon*
*33. KENYON, JAMES B. *The Industrialization of the Skokie Area*
*34. PHILLIPS, PAUL GROUNDS. *The Hashemite Kingdom of Jordan: Prolegomena to a Technical Assistance Program*
*35. CARMIN, ROBERT LEIGHTON. *Anápolis, Brazil: Regional Capital of an Agricultural Frontier*
36. GOLD, ROBERT N. *Manufacturing Structure and Pattern of the South Bend–Mishawaka Area* 1954. 224 pp. 6 folded inserts. 2 maps in pocket.
*37. SISCO, PAUL HARDEMAN. *The Retail Function of Memphis*
*38. VAN DONGEN, IRENE S. *The British East African Transport Complex*
*39. FRIEDMANN, JOHN R. P. *The Spatial Structure of Economic Development in the Tennessee Valley*
*40. GROTEWOLD, ANDREAS. *Regional Changes in Corn Production in the United States from 1909 to 1949*
*41. BJORKLUND, E. M. *Focus on Adelaide—Functional Organization of the Adelaide Region, Australia*
*42. FORD, ROBERT N. *A Resource Use Analysis and Evaluation of the Everglades Agricultural Area*
*43. CHRISTENSEN, DAVID E. *Rural Occupance in Transition: Sumter and Lee Counties, Georgia*
*44. GUZMÁN, LOUIS E. *Farming and Farmlands in Panama*

* Out of print.

*45. ZADROZNY, MITCHELL G. *Water Utilization in the Middle Mississippi Valley*

*46. AHMED, G. MUNIR. *Manufacturing Structure and Pattern of Waukegan–North Chicago*

47. RANDALL, DARRELL. *Factors of Economic Development and the Okovango Delta*
1956. 282 pp. (Research Paper No. 3, Program of Education and Research in Planning, The University of Chicago.)

48. BOXER, BARUCH. *Israeli Shipping and Foreign Trade* 1957. 176 pp.

49. MAYER, HAROLD M. *The Port of Chicago and the St. Lawrence Seaway* 1957. 283 pp.

50. PATTISON, WILLIAM D. *Beginnings of the American Rectangular Land Survey System, 1784–1800*
1957. 2d printing 1963. 260 pp.

*51. BROWN, ROBERT HAROLD. *Political Areal-Functional Organization: With Special Reference to St. Cloud, Minnesota*

*52. BEYER, JACQUELYN. *Integration of Grazing and Crop Agriculture: Resources Management Problems in the Uncompahgre Valley Irrigation Project*

53. ACKERMAN, EDWARD A. *Geography as a Fundamental Research Discipline* 1958. 40 pp. $1.00.

*54. AL-KHASHAB, WAFIQ HUSSAIN. *The Water Budget of the Tigris and Euphrates Basin*

*55. LARIMORE, ANN EVANS. *The Alien Town: Patterns of Settlement in Busoga, Uganda*

56. MURPHY, FRANCIS C. *Regulating Flood-Plain Development* 1958. 216 pp.

*57. WHITE, GILBERT F., *et al. Changes in Urban Occupance of Flood Plains in the United States*

*58. COLBY, MARY MC RAE. *The Geographic Structure of Southeastern North Carolina*

*59. MEGEE, MARY CATHERINE. *Monterrey, Mexico: Internal Patterns and External Relations*

60. WEBER, DICKINSON. *A Comparison of Two Oil City Business Centers (Odessa-Midland, Texas)*
1958. 256 pp.

61. PLATT, ROBERT S. *Field Study in American Geography* 1959. 408 pp.

62. GINSBURG, NORTON, editor. *Essays on Geography and Economic Development* 1960. 196 pp.

63. HARRIS, CHAUNCY D., and FELLMANN, JEROME D. *International List of Geographical Serials*
1960. 247 pp.

*64. TAAFFE, ROBERT N. *Rail Transportation and the Economic Development of Soviet Central Asia*

*65. SHEAFFER, JOHN R. *Flood Proofing: An Element in a Flood Damage Reduction Program*

66. RODGERS, ALLAN L. *The Industrial Geography of the Port of Genova* 1960. 150 pp.

67. KENYON, JAMES B. *Industrial Localization and Metropolitan Growth: The Paterson-Passaic District* 1960. 250 pp.

68. GINSBURG, NORTON. *An Atlas of Economic Development*
1961. 119 pp. 14 × 8½″. Cloth $7.50. University of Chicago Press.

69. CHURCH, MARTHA. *Spatial Organization of Electric Power Territories in Massachusetts*
1960. 200 pp.

70. WHITE, GILBERT F., *et al. Papers on Flood Problems* 1961. 234 pp.

71. GILBERT, E. W. *The University Town in England and West Germany*
1961. 79 pp. 4 plates. 30 maps and diagrams.

72. BOXER, BARUCH. *Ocean Shipping in the Evolution of Hong Kong* 1961. 108 pp.

73. ROBINSON, IRA M. *New Industrial Towns on Canada's Resource Frontier*
1962. (Research Paper No. 4, Program of Education and Research in Planning, The University of Chicago.) 192 pp.

74. TROTTER, JOHN E. *State Park System in Illinois* 1962. 152 pp.

75. BURTON, IAN. *Types of Agricultural Occupance of Flood Plains in the United States*
1962. 167 pp.

76. PRED, ALLAN. *The External Relations of Cities During 'Industrial Revolution'* 1962. 124 pp.

77. BARROWS, HARLAN H. *Lectures on the Historical Geography of the United States as Given in 1933*
Edited by WILLIAM A. KOELSCH. 1962. 248 pp.

78. KATES, ROBERT WILLIAM. *Hazard and Choice Perception in Flood Plain Management*
1962. 157 pp.

79. HUDSON, JAMES. *Irrigation Water Use in the Utah Valley, Utah* 1962. 249 pp.

80. ZELINSKY, WILBUR. *A Bibliographic Guide to Population Geography* 1962. 257 pp.

*81. DRAINE, EDWIN H. *Import Traffic of Chicago and Its Hinterland*

*82. KOLARS, JOHN F. *Tradition, Season, and Change in a Turkish Village*

83. WIKKRAMATILEKE, RUDOLPH. *Southeast Ceylon: Trends and Problems in Agricultural Settlement*
1963. 163 pp.

84. KANSKY, K. J. *Structure of Transportation Networks: Relationships between Network Geometry and Regional Characteristics* 1963. 155 pp.

85. BERRY, BRIAN J. L. *Commercial Structure and Commercial Blight* 1963. 254 pp.

86. BERRY, BRIAN J. L., and TENNANT, ROBERT J. *Chicago Commercial Reference Handbook*
1963. 278 pp.

87. BERRY, BRIAN J. L., and HANKINS, THOMAS D. *A Bibliographic Guide to the Economic Regions of the United States* 1963. 128 pp.

88. MARCUS, MELVIN G. *Climate-Glacier Studies in the Juneau Ice Field Region, Alaska* 1964. 128 pp.

89. SMOLE, WILLIAM J. *Owner-Cultivatorship in Middle Chile* 1964. 176 pp.

90. HELVIG, MAGNE. *Chicago's External Truck Movements: Spatial Interaction between the Chicago Area and Its Hinterland* 1964. 132 pp.

* Out of print.